Calvin Blanchard

**Religio-Political Physics**

Calvin Blanchard

**Religio-Political Physics**

ISBN/EAN: 9783337375805

Printed in Europe, USA, Canada, Australia, Japan

Cover: Foto ©Suzi / pixelio.de

More available books at **www.hansebooks.com**

# RELIGIO-POLITICAL PHYSICS:

OR,

# THE SCIENCE AND ART

OF

## MAN'S DELIVERANCE

FROM

### IGNORANCE-ENGENDERED MYSTICISM,

AND ITS RESULTING

## THEO-MORAL QUACKERY

AND

## GOVERNMENTAL BRIGANDAGE.

### BY CALVIN BLANCHARD.

---

"Nature is all-sufficient; man's *fancied* "supernatural" longing is her index to the perfection to which development, including science and art, irrepressibly tend. All evil is consequent on ignorance, skepticism and despair, with respect to the power of the substantial, through spontaneity and *practical* organization, and combination, to complete the *all-important* half of its undertaking; to create supply, adequate to demand; to inaugurate Heaven on Earth."—*Religion of Science.*

---

NEW YORK:
PUBLISHED BY C. BLANCHARD, 76 NASSAU STREET.
COMMON ERA, 1861.

# READ THIS BOOK!

If you are not *quite sure* that perfection in religious knowledge was achieved eighteen hundred and sixty years ago, READ THIS BOOK!

If you are not *entirely contented* with the practical working of moralism, for the particulars of which, consult the world's daily records, READ THIS BOOK!

If you happen to have ever so slight misgivings with respect to the *reality* of the freedom which "elective franchise" secures, READ THIS BOOK!

If you are not *irredeemably pledged* to the horrid delusion that man is the inextricably doomed victim of mystery-religion, self-crucifying morality, and monarchy, aristocracy, or majority-tyranny, READ THIS BOOK!

If you have not irrevocably pronounced it *impossible* that *physical* science and art can eliminate mystical, indeterminate speculation from religion and law, as completely as they have thrust such vexatious charlatanry from so many lower natural departments, READ THIS BOOK!

If you believe in the development-theory of creation, and behold in *Nature* THE ALL—SUFFICIENT, READ THIS BOOK!

# § 1. INTRODUCTORY.

No truths can be more evident than that mankind *universally* have a right to all that they are constituted to desire, and that nature can grant it.

To deny this is to insult justice, blaspheme the only Almighty that we can *know anything about*, and fall back on natural depravity, and the whole scheme of anthropomorphitic theology, including vicarious sacrifice, temporal "punishment" for "crime," and "eternal" "vengeance" for "sin."

But man's claim to *perfect* and *sufficiently lasting* happiness, or *complete* liberty, *necessarily* involves certain conditions to be by him fulfilled. For if man could *miraculously* have whatever he wished for, he would find that he could wish for nothing that would not be perfectly insipid at first, and intolerably nauseous immediately thereafter. "*Eternal*" and *unconditional* happiness, to be enjoyed *without organs*, is the most absurd fancy that human folly ever tried to entertain; and *everlasting* consciousness would necessarily be, at best, but perpetual *ennui* to all beings not wholly destitute of *sense*.

The mutual functions of the priests of religion and officers of government self-evidently should be, to study human and lower material nature, and thence deduce a civil constitution and body of law; and in accordance with these, *organize* man so that he can *assist* development, *direct* progress, so harmoniously *modify*, and powerfully and advantageously *combine* his own force and that of all else in his connection as to produce such a condition of things that to desire will be to have, with but the intervention of just exertion enough to give due value to possession, and prolong his conscious existence, under these circumstances, till all the varieties of happiness presentable to the five senses exhaust their value by repetition. All religion that aims beyond this is *delusion*. All government that aims short of this is *failure*.

In consequence of religion and government lacking this *intelligible* and *practical* aim, man, bewildered by mystery, has been the dupe of sacerdotal fraud, and the victim of political quackery and experimenting.

As all evil is *physical*, spiritual prescriptions are quackery. As all man's cravings are for *material* good, " immateriality " cannot satisfy them. As no sane person can voluntarily act except from selfish motives, "disinterestedness" is a fallacy, "duty" and "conscience" are most treacherous snares, and moral codes are perfect abortions.

The religious aspirations are the premonitory symptoms that nature, whose cerebrum or *positive* organ of highest thought manifests them, is pregnant with perfection. Man is nature's forehead, the lower animals are her backhead.

Skepticism is the last analysis of abstraction—the most absurd of all absurdities—the most inane of inanities.

That theo-religio-fungus—Protestantism, and its resulting *popular* free discussion of religion, are *not causes,* but *mere incidental accompaniments* of human advancement. They compose the fifth wheel of the car of progress, the empty rattling and singular appearance of which monopolize vulgar notice.

Freedom of thought, of speech, and of the press, like praying and moralizing, can do *no more* toward *actually* freeing or *benefiting* mankind, than they can toward liberating the action of a watch, steam-engine, or spinning-jenny, which don't work freely, because the parts are not fitted to each other, or harmoniously, and in a workmanlike manner, related.

So long as religion is a mysterious puzzle, law will be a vexatious mockery; order, a subterfuge for tyranny; government, an arbitrary imposition; liberty, an illusion; right, a fiction; justice, an exile; peace, a mere armistice; and happiness, *non est inventus.*

Union and organization alone can give strength; strength, freedom; freedom, happiness. But union and organization must be for good instead of for evil. All power is capable of abuse in exact proportion as it is capable of use. No power can be *absolutely* destroyed, or even rendered indifferent.

Theological vagaries and absurdities, political folly, quackery, and fraud, and governmental brigandage, waste and profligacy cannot cease, till education is reorganized on an *objective* basis, the claims of labor, skill and capital equitably adjusted, the affections emancipated, woman liberated and enthroned as the object of man's adoration,* children's rights to the perfect development that science, art, and lower nature can give them, secured, human law based on physics, faith strengthened past wavering, and

* See "Religion of Science," p. 127, and "Essence of Science," pp. 81-2.

transferred from miracle to development—reposed in the ministers of the science of sciences and art of arts, instead of in the priests of mystery and superstition, or instead of being destroyed, or sacrificed on the altar of skepticism—till nature, including science and art, is looked up to as *The All-Sufficient.*

## § 2.  INCONSISTENCY AND INCOMPETENCY OF PRESENT RELIGION AND GOVERNMENT.

Democracy in America is an awkward and servile imitation of the theo-governmental polity which monarchical Europe mainly begged from barbaric Asia, who learned it in schools as savage as those which ignorance now keeps in the most heathenish regions of Africa.  " Our free institutions," apart from the little *physical* science and art that have become *stealthily* interwoven therein, are absurd and futile attempts to build the temple of liberty with the same kind of materials as those which compose the dungeon of despotism, with the mortifying exception, that they are in the last stage of decay.

Daniel Webster, and other eminent American jurists, have correctly decided that the government of the United States, notwithstanding its *constitutional* divorcement from religion, is, *essentially,* Christian ; in truth, a surreptitious or " left-handed " theocracy.*

Lord Macaulay glorifies those *avowed* unions of Church and State—monarchies and aristocracies—for being more efficient than democracies, in preserving a civilization which superabundantly piles the world's wealth into the hands of a few, and degrades the majority of mankind to " a multitude of people, none of whom have had more than half a breakfast, or expect to have more than half a dinner." †

* See Webster's plea in the Girard will case.
† See Macaulay's letter to Henry S. Randall, author of the " Life of Jefferson."

The magistrate for the county of Berks, in England, has communicated to the " London Times " of December 10, 1860, a statement respecting the condition of the peasantry in nineteen towns and villages, as " *a fair sample of the condition of the agricultural laboring population of England.*" A mere synopsis of the details of this statement would occupy about three pages of this work. They are as horrible and revolting as words can describe, or even imagination paint ; they come fully up, or rather *down*, to what Eugene Sue describes in " The Mysteries of Paris." " Our peasantry," remarks the " Times " on this communication, " *are far worse lodged than our beasts of burden.*" Besides the worse than beastly lodging, and starvation and nakedness to match, parents and adult children, and brothers and sisters men and women grown, crowdedly sleep in the same room, and often in the same bed together " *pell-mell,*" and

James Buchanan, whose presidency over this nation terminates in the year of grace one thousand eight hundred and sixty-one, in his last annual Message, extols Democracy as "the noblest system of government ever devised by mortals;" meaning, as is evident from the theological bearing of all he says in the connection, that the government of the United States is the best ever founded on subjectivity, moralism, or any phase of the theologic phantasm.

In his magniloquent bunkum, the President is sustained by the unanimous "whoraws" of that overwhelming but uncritical and easily led portion of mankind which composes "the masses" (and whom it will be easier to lead right than wrong as soon as their leaders understand their own true interests), and by the opinions, *as far as expressed*, of all his predecessors; none of whom seem to have had more than a glimmering idea of any other than a subjective, speculative, moralistic, supernaturalistic, *arbitrary* foundation for the government of mankind.

But President Buchanan frankly admits and sorely laments that the *practical operation* of "the noblest system of government ever devised by mortals," has been to bring the Union, of which it is the cement, into the very throes of dissolution, only eighty-four years after its formation!

"The noblest system of government ever devised by mortals" has a currency so fluctuating that property is as insecure, and business as risky, as they can possibly be; and that currency is so inflated, that it cheats the people into that most mischievous fallacy, that it is better to import than to manufacture; and plunges them into the folly of raising corn, cotton, and infernal tobacco, and sending them three or four thousand miles to market, and of distilling whisky at forty cents a gallon, to be poisoned in France, and sent back again as brandy, at from four to eight dollars a gallon, when they might raise the pure wine and brandy producing grape, and have, within five or ten miles, a ready

---

some daughters have as many as four bastards. And this is *Protestant, Christian* England! This is *moral* England! This is England, the very bulwark of *holy matrimony!* This is England that has *abolished slavery!* This is England that cants so edifyingly about French licentiousness! This is *the* England that is more afraid than any nation on earth (except Puritanical Scotland, that has more bastards and drunkards, in proportion to its inhabitants, than has any other country) that if *marital* bondage was abolished, or even loosened, *promiscuous intercourse and licentiousness would result!*

And "Britannia rules the waves," and the sun never sets on her empire, but may that sun speedily shine his last on all such mockeries of religion, law justice, government, and civilization.

market for the numerous products which a well-regulated currency would employ home industry upon, besides abolishing that suction-pipe of political thieves, the tariff.

"The noblest system of government ever devised by mortals" plunged the United States into universal bankruptcy only sixty-one years after its inauguration; and from the very first, it has tormented the millions who, as inhabitants of the said States, have reposed faith in it, with a constant succession of "panics."

And finally, the damning truth defies contradiction, that throughout the vast region wherein prevails "the noblest system of government ever devised by mortals," all the labor is performed by "wages-slaves" and "chattel-slaves;" the best judges cannot decide which are most miserable; and people of superior benevolence and understanding contend that both slaves and masters are equally entitled to pity.*

In view of all this, I hope that the *reflecting* portion of mankind, to whom alone I appeal, will not accuse me of temerity in claiming, as I do, to have discovered a substitute, by which it will be incalculably advantageous to displace not only monarchy and aristocracy as at present constituted, but even "the noblest system of government ever devised by mortals," in Mr. Buchanan's estimation.

"The *noblest* system of government," I shall demonstrate, will be one that will make liberty *perfect* and *actual*, extend it to all, physically prepare the whole earth for it, and "enlarge the area of freedom" from pole to pole.

That the government of the United States is *really* the

---

* Those who uphold chattel-slavery are perfectly consistent with respect to those who oppose it in favor of wages-slavery, or who do not look to an entire reorganization of the social and governmental polity of the world. Would not the slave-trade, if *provisionally* regulated, instead of vainly opposed and driven into its self-preservative horrors, be a boon to the African, rescued from immolation on the altar of savage warfare, or even kidnapped from his horrible brutality? Are the plantation negroes and negresses of the South, or the hod-carriers, under-ground steam-engine tenders, and seamstresses of the North least miserable? And was the chattel-slave revolution of Hayti, or the wages-slave revolution of France, the most sanguinary? In spite of the navies of all civilized nations, the slave-trade is vigorously kept up. A great number of new slave vessels are annually fitted up at the New York ship yards even. These hell-craft, in order to escape detection and elude pursuit, have to be so built that about twenty per cent. of their human cargoes die of suffocation. Often, to avoid capture, their officers and crew run them aground in the night, escape to the shore in boats, and leave sometimes as many as five hundred chained negroes to perish with the wreck. This, together with the suffocation horror abovementioned, *regulating* and *licensing* the slave-trade would have prevented.

very opposite of what it is "*constitutionally*" and *specu-latively*, will sufficiently appear from the following speci-men of the choice theological and most *unconstitutional* morsels with which the late message of that greatest of all sticklers for "*The* Constitution," President Buchanan, is interspersed; "My prayer to God is, that he would preserve the Constitution and the Union."

"*The* Union" has, *constitutionally*, insulted all the min-isters of "God," and given "God" himself to understand that it don't care its smallest coin for him or his "religion." It flatly tells him that its "Congress shall make no law respecting an establishment of religion." Yet the President coolly asks "God" to "preserve the Constitution and the Union!"

This decidedly beats the presumptuousness of the man who, one cold, stormy night, being pressed by sudden neces-sity, made a most abominable use of the portico of a house belonging to a gentleman whom, together with his whole family, he had most grossly and publicly insulted, hurriedly rang the bell, and importunately demanded a leaf of the family Bible; but *did not* carry his impudence so far as to insist that his repudiated friend should apply the sacred paper to the vile office for which it was required.

In further proof of what a jumble of treachery and hum-bug "*The* Constitution" is, I will call the reader's atten-tion to the fact that the President aforesaid has, since the promulgation of his said theological Message, issued a Pro-clamation, stuck as brim full of the very "religion" that "*The* Constitution" is specially aimed against, as any pope's bull apostolical could possibly be, appointing a day of "fasting, humiliation, and prayer," and abandoning "the Union," "Constitution," and all, to their repudiated "God," in these terms: "God's arm only can save us from the awful effects of our own crimes and follies—our own ingrati-tude and guilt toward our Heavenly Father."

In the name of all that is not stark staring madness or slavering idiocy, I ask, has not this nation had enough of humiliation? Bullies and blackguards are prominently among its high functionaries; during the present and several preceding administrations, official thieves have run away with no inconsiderable amount of its funds; swindlers, both "elected" and appointed, have revelled in its treasury, and its next President, or head distributer of spoils, has been chosen to that honorable office, on the strength of his having been a soldier in the Black Hawk War, a common laborer on a farm, a roller of logs in a saw-mill, and a rail-splitter; the last qualification being trumpeted as the most important of all; it unquestionably secured his election so far as the *popular* vote was concerned.

And are not the people to whom the aforesaid Proclamation is addressed, in a fair way, thanks to demagogism, to have enough of the virtue of fasting, without being specially exhorted thereunto? And is not this presidential conduct, both in *fact*, and more especially in *manner*, contrary to the very spirit of "*The* Constitution?"

Can't the weakest noddle outside of Bedlam perceive that "*The* Constitution" is a weathercock that readily turns whichever way the breath of demagogism, cant, and humbug blows?

Mr. Buchanan is certainly one of the most expert gamesters that ever shuffled those convenient cards—the people—though he is sorely put to his trumps, and makes some grave mistakes during the latter end of his game. But I candidly ask those *who are gifted with a capacity for reflection at all uncommon*, if his Proclamation does not bear fifty marks of having emanated from a negro Methodist camp-meeting, to one of having come from the head of a government, the union between which and the church has been dissolved? Let any one who has a voice attuned to *bass* cant, read that Proclamation, appropriately intersperse it with Methodistic groans, amen-ers and glory-to-God-ers, and see if I have overrated its sanctimoniousness.

All remember the great Swartwout robbery, and, during the last four years, the following specimens of political smartness stick out so prominently as to come instantly to mind: the Fort Snelling job diddled the people out of $400,000; Willett's Point do., $150,000; New Bedford Fort Site do., $30,000; Utah Flour Contract do., $160,000; Utah Corn Contract do., $270,000; Utah Mule Sale do., $240,000; El Paso Wagon Road do., $200,000; Fowler Defalcation do., $175,000; Godard Bailey's Robbery do., $870,000. Add to these the millions on millions of expenses not here enumerated, of the Mormon Expedition, got up on purpose to give army contracts, etc., etc., etc., to those who had done party service, for which no other subterfuge could be devised for rewarding, and say if "The Union" is not sufficiently humiliated.

Until "Old Buck," "Old Abe," or some of their successors in the chair of state, issue a proclamation recommending that the word "*consistency*" be expurgated from the dictionary, or that the first clause of the first Article of the "Amendments to The Constitution" be stricken out, "The Model Republic" will justly be the laughing-stock, not only of the more intelligent portion of mankind, but of the broken-down theological dynasty of Rome itself.

Let me not be understood to insinuate even, that President Buchanan is not as consistent as were any of his predecessors, except Washington, whom an unfortunate train of events compelled to take the lead in founding our theo-democratic Utopia; and as "conscientious" a man as has occupied the White House since the abominable political theory that "to the victors belong the spoils," has been in full practice.

"Old Buck" rode into the Presidency on a hobby foaled of that most speculative of abstractions—"*The* Constitution." "Old Abe" rode in on a rail. And the difference between their administrations, *other things being equal*, will be precisely the odds between fiddlededum and fiddlededee. And this rule will hold good with respect to the comparative merits of any two presidents that have held, or may hold office under theo-democratic constitutionalism.

But let us hope and strive that the last Proclamation of the President, and the recent Bull of the Pope may be among the last vestiges of the Dark Ages. I say *among* the last, for Pius IX. *may* be foolish enough to let loose another hornless Bull, and it is hardly possible but that pious "Old Abe" will, in order not to be outdone in anything by "Old Buck," give our religious putridity another stirring up, and our bogus Constitution another besmearing with the rotten theology which essentially composes our counterfeit democracy.

Whilst the United States is, religiously, the common slush-tub for excrescent supernaturalism, whilst the first clause of the first Article of "Amendments to the The Constitution" remains, and so long as our chief magistrates continue to issue such Messages and Proclamations as they have in the main hitherto done, why not give them their full titles?—to wit: President of The United States, Chief Priest of Unconstitutional Religion, Wholesale Dealer in Contraband Christianity, and Defender, Protector and Preserver of Dilapidated Episcopacy and Third-hand Popery.

It being late at night when I finished writing the last sentence, I reclined back in my chair for a recess, fell asleep, and dreamed that I was translated to the twenty-first century. Everything was astonishingly improved. As the readiest method of finding out how, I opened a dictionary bearing that date, and read :

*Constitution*—The embodiment of science, or system of physics, on which government or human law is based. Formerly, during the age of metaphysical absurdity, opinionism, speculative abstraction, and religio-political obfuscation, the main cord of that infernally vexatious entanglement in utter disregard of meaning called law; into the meshes of which, those most wily and dangerous of all knaves, politicians, wheedled man, when he was only "civilized," and therefore excessively verdant, to *confine himself;* ostensibly, that he might not run wild, or otherwise abuse his boasted right to "the *pursuit* of happiness;" but really, that they might swindle, and plunder, and insult him with impunity. "*The* Constitution" was, of course, the darling theme and favorite hobby of theo-democratic bandits of all parties. It was the common scape-goat of stupendous fraud and gigantic wrong. *Imaginarily*, (on the part of the masses,) the *guaranty for free government!* *Really*, the height of political folly. *Essentially*, gammon. The Social Organism never endured constitutionalism, and its coöppression, "elective franchise," long at a time. It frantically chose even military dictatorship, in its stead.

## § 3   GENERAL VIEW OF THE PHYSICAL FOUNDATION FOR PRACTICAL RELIGION AND ACTUAL FREEDOM.

Man will be the victim of theo-religio-political anarchy and oppression, and the dupe of mystery, metaphysics, and their resulting Utopianism, till religion (necessarily the theory to which government must, openly or *sub rosâ*, be the practice) is a combination of science, as fast as developed, for the perfection of man and all lower materiality in the connection, up to the point to which nature, through the highest human aspiration, manifests her aim; and till, to this science of sciences, government corresponds as the art of arts; till, through development, and the modification and combination of human* and other substantial power, law becomes, to every member of the Social Organism, what gravitation is to the celestial spheroids which compose the Solar System—a *perfecter* and *insurer* of order and *actual* freedom. But I shall treat this vast subject somewhat specially, and with reference to measures *immediately* to be taken, in its proper place. In the meantime, I pledge myself to advance no theory which I shall not demonstrate to be practical—none that is not indispensably necessary to be understood before the inauguration of *true* religion, and *actually* free government, can be successfully undertaken.

All government that has ever existed has been mere short-sighted, make-shift polity ; what is most lyingly called democracy, or elective government, is peculiarly so; any polity that should look beyond *present emergency*, the necessarily special-minded multitude, *misled by demagogues*, would sneer at as "mere theory." Popular government is therefore a constant succession of changes without alteration for the better, but for the worse, at the rapid rate in which continual shifting impoverishes. If nature had formed all mankind, or even " the majority," equally capable of knowing, *à priori*, or before trial, what *national* measures would be best, that common phrase—" the masses "—would have no significancy.

*Equality* is the Procrustean opponent of every *organic* thing in nature. *Equality*, nature abhors exactly in proportion to the difference between the Sun and the smallest satellite in his *free* EMPIRE. *Equality*, therefore, is the roughest shod hobby on which the most brutal and unrelenting tyrants—the most insatiate political brigands—ever trampled down human rights.

To what a rotten condition *equality* has brought government, in the United States, during the short period in the life of a nation of only eighty-four years. Our *equality*-nursed Social Organism has, almost from the first, groaned panic, bankruptcy, defalcation, corruption, and repudiation of contracts : and now it shrieks dissolution.

The world wants a government, the freedom and stability of which shall correspond to the freedom and stability that characterize the spheroids of which the Solar *Empire* is composed ; and I shall demonstrate that this is not only possible, but the only government that *can* be *established ;* that can *be* government ; that can *put an end to anarchy.*

## § 4. THE TRIUNE THEOLOGICAL MYSTERY NATURALLY SOLVED.

" God is something more than a mere moral order of the world, and has quite another and a more living motive power in himself than is ascribed to him by the jejune subtilty of abstract idealists. Why then dost thou shrink from naming the nature of God by its true name? Evidently only because thou hast a general horror of things in their truth and reality; because thou lookest at all things through the deceptive vapors of mysticism."—*Feuerbach's Essence of Christianity.*

" Man cannot even desire miracle-happiness; the " supernatural " does not bear thinking of; its very wording involves as many contradictions as statements—as many absurdities as propositions."

" The existence of mind, apart from its positive and negative *substantial* requisites, is inconceivable. An 'immaterial' Heaven could be of no value to material man, or even to what he egotistically assumes to be *his* mind or 'spirit,' admitting that that function of brain and coöperating materiality could exist ' disembodied.' "—*Religion of Science.*

Materiality (always bearing in mind its capacity for development, including science and art) is adequate to all for which miracle can be *conceivably* invoked. Human and lower *natural* forces, through the harmonious modification and all-powerful combinations of which they are susceptible, are competent to solve the liberty problem—to clear up the immortality-enigma—to inaugurate Heaven on Earth.*

Matter is *God the Almighty Father*, Man is *God the best beloved Son*—one with the Father—nature's highest organ of mind—her cerebrum.

Mind is *God the Holy Ghost*—the Sanctifier or Sanc-

* I must gratefully acknowledge, that to that embodiment of science— "The Positive Philosophy " of Auguste Comte—I am indebted for a clear conception of the all-sufficiency of nature. Before studying that, I considered man the inextricable dupe of priestcraft, and the shuttlecock of theo-monarchical and theo-democratical violence, oppression, and spoliation. Comte himself did not know what a foundation he had laid,* as is evident from the incompatible religio-political superstructure that he arbitrarily and speculatively raised thereon. This is but natural. The wonder would have been, had *one* intellect proved sufficient to the task of not only discovering the foundation, but of laying out the plan of the temple of true liberty. The emissaries of superstition give " The Positive Philosophy " as wide a berth as the captain of the most unseaworthy vessel would give a lee-shore in a storm ; but they dwell with peculiar delight and most infernal cowardice on Comte's " Positive Religion " and " Positive Politics ;" with respect to which that just appreciator ot Comte *himself*—Mr. G. H. Lewes—amiably remarks: " Over his (Comte's) subsequent efforts to found a social doctrine, and to become the founder of a new religion, let us draw a veil. They are unfortunate attempts which remind us of Bacon's scientific investigations ; and, in the minds of many, these unfortunate attempts will create a prejudice against what is truly grand in his philosophic career. In the 'Cours de Philosophie Positive' ('Positive Philosophy') we have the grandest, because on the whole the truest, system which Philosophy has yet produced; nor should any differences, which must inevitably arise on points of detail, make us forget the greatness of the achievement and the debt we owe to the lonely thinker who wrought out this system." —*Lewes' Biographical History of Philosophy ;* (published by D. Appleton & Co. " The Positive Philosophy " is published by C. Blanchard.)

* Comte laid the foundation whereon to realize those magnificent conceptions of Fourier— the equitable adjustment of the claims of labor, skill, and capital, and passional emancipation. But the task was too mighty for the intellectual organs of any one man to perform with impunity. Fourier, like Comte, Bacon, Kepler, and so many other intellectual giants, strained his organs of thought, and committed vagaries in minor "points of detail;" and science and art will continue to have their martyrs till human emancipation is complete. Fourier's great work, " The Social Destiny of Man," is published by C. Blanchard.

tioner—functional of the Father and the Son, and necessarily one with them.

God the Son will be crucified to take away the sin of the
world—he will be in antagonistic or *crosswise* connection
with everything till, through that only conceivable miracle—
development; through all human and lower material force
harmoniously liberated and most advantageously combined
for good, earth shall be transformed to Heaven.   Then, God
the Son will sit *glorified*, at the *right*, instead of, as now, at
the *wrong* side of God the Father, and God the Holy Ghost
will, of course, be perfectly satisfied, and sanction or sanctify
all.   Then, that subterfuge of ignorance, that lounge of mental laziness—the great supernatural, supersensible God and
Father of inexplicable mystery, unintelligible balderdash,
and unsurpassable folly, will be eliminated.   Then, the puz-
zling abstraction that is now worshipped as the Almighty, and
the wretched mockery of religion immediately consequent
thereon, will, like the arch which the stone-mason forms in
*imagination*, and the *provisional* wooden one which he consequently erects, be superseded by the substantial and
efficient.

Man's holiness-befogged or "heavenly" desires are the
very quintessence of sensuousness; they are nothing more,
and nothing less, than substantial nature's drafts on development, which will most assuredly be paid, and in the very
currency which *alone can* discharge them, when legally presented—when presented in the only way that could make
their payment *value received*.   Yet man, deceived by his
unworthy agents in the case—the bogus priesthood, or false
clergy—mopes through the world, panic-stricken, and
reviling nature as a bankrupt, with the keys to her ample
treasury actually in his possession; too discouraged to *try* to
*practically* use them; thinking it "too good to be true,"
that he has the *intelligible* means whereby to open and find
all that he can *really* wish for.

Let any one whose rationality in the matter of religion has
not been completely subverted, compare my exposition of
the "three in one and one in three," with *any* other, and
candidly say which can be best *understand*.   Nay, I chal-
lenge all believers in "supernaturalism" to say, upon oath,
if any expositions of "The Trinity," in accordance with
*their* creed, are sufficient to hang a thought upon.

The Jews, from whom Christians acknowledge that they
received all they pretend to know about God the Father,
deny all knowledge of this God's eternal Son.   And it was

only eighteen hundred years ago, according to the *Christian* record, that anything was ever *spoken* concerning the third partner in the theological firm—the Holy Ghost.

Those who are curious with respect to the minutia of "supernaturalism," I refer to the "Devil's Pulpit," by Robert Taylor, and to that most profound work on Mythology, "The Life of Jesus Critically Examined," by Dr. David Friedrich Strauss, a work which, says Theodore Parker, is "the most formidable assailant of the ecclesiastical theology of Christendom."

But those for whom these pages are *specially* intended, need not be told that all the *dramatis personæ* in the great farce of man's supernatural creation, burlesque fall, parsimonious redemption, and wholesale damnation, are but mistakes, personifications, and myths. All gospel preachers, even, except the thickest skulled brawlers, let out this secret to such of their hearers as have brains to *comprehend*.

Of all supernatural *personages*, the Devil is surely the one in whom there is most reason to believe. Even in orthodox estimation, he is "the God of this world." His armies crowd the "broad road," whilst the followers of his opponent, only "here and there" dot the "narrow path." Yet the Rev. Henry Ward Beecher says, that "mirthfulness has exorcised the Devil a hundred times!"

So! There goes the Devil! A summary disposition of his Dread Majesty! Well, *I* comprehend, *I* "take," *I* enjoy the fun of the thing. But, Sir, the majority of your congregation evidently do not understand that the black, cloven-footed, long-tailed monster who populates Hell, and on whose account God's Son was crucified, is only a fit of *hypochondriasis!*—a mere "blue devil" that Jo Miller or W. E. Burton could beat you, or Jesus Christ either, all to nothing in "casting out."

Your jokes, sir, would be very serious ones for yourself, were they universally comprehended, unless you chose to turn right about, and preach the new gospel of science, instead of the worn-out, devil-spell of mystery. Come, now; do but this, and I'll take one thousand dollars' worth of shares in your new meeting-house to begin with; devote myself wholly to the church, and espouse the cause of all the clergy who follow your example, with *more* energy, if possible, than I have ever opposed theo-deviltry, or religio-political swindling.

Some of your puns, though good, are still much inferior

to those of an ordinary clown in a circus, that any gloomy demoniac can enjoy the benefit of for twenty-five cents; and if your congregation *generally* understood *the drift* of them, depend upon it, they would soon cease to pay you anything like five thousand dollars a year for them.

If "the Devil" signifies the dumps, why may not the everlastingly spiteful "Holy Ghost" personify the sulks; "Christ" be a myth, "God" a nullity, "divine revelation" the mutual bantling of ignorance and imposture, and all who preach it, either swindlers or blunderheads? Why not?

Apropos of demonology, I will say to all those of whom the Devil has taken possession in consequence of gormandizing or eating late suppers—"fast;" and "pray" your convivial friends not to "lead you into temptation." I don't claim to be the *sole* author of this prescription; for, with but slight alteration, as all who have read the Evangelists will perceive, 'tis as old as that wine-bibbing metamorphosis of Bacchus called Christ, on whom is fathered so many queer parables or conundrums, and to whom is falsely attributed the choicest *bon-mots* of Zoroaster, Plato and Confucius.

Strange that "infidels" do not perceive, that if the multitude were capable of *investigating* a subject as abstruse as religion, the atheism of *all the intelligent preachers*, and the little pains they take to disguise it, would be quite sufficient to convert them to *mere unbelievers*.

Clergymen of talent, I implore you to abandon a system that you are evidently so ashamed of that you cannot but despise yourselves for advocating, and *openly* and *fully* preach *the religion of science*. Oh, if you would but do this, how soon man would *have* the Millennium that he now but faintly dreams of. And your salaries would increase instead of diminishing, your situations would be perfectly secure, provided you had the requisite qualifications to fulfill them, and your influence would be supreme; all which I shall demonstrate further on.

## § 5. OUR THEO-POLITICAL CHAOS.

The most advanced States throughout the world are openly or *sub rosâ*, united with, and subordinated to, a Church, the fundamental dogma of which was promulgated by man when he was in his primitive savageness, and necessarily so inexperienced that the most correct judgment by him formable, could be no other than the most erroneous one imaginable; when *pure* conjecture was the *only* practicability—the *sole* alternative to *utter* doubt: when the only *possible* religious theory was that monstrous assumption, at variance with *all* experience—the anthropomorphitic phantasm;* according to which, that mere subjective and objective, positive and negative function of cerebral and coöperating external materiality—the will, is almighty, and independent of substantiality.

The doctrines resulting from such a premise are now, of course, in monstrous contrast with nineteenth century science and art; they are practically dead,† worse than useless, and held beneath contempt by all people of more than ordinary understanding. The higher clergy preach them for salary, as the more intelligent and scientific members of society, when they condescend to hear them, do so for patronage. "Smart preachers" are so ashamed of the faith they *profess*, that in their anxiety to make known their unbelief in it to their hearers *whose mental comprehensions are general, and above the ordinary calibre*, they barely disguise their infidelity from those whose *critical acumen is naturally, appropriately, and necessarily confined to specialities*—from the most unreasonably despised, insultingly flattered and cajoled, and abominably abused multitude, by whom both themselves and their decoys aforesaid are sustained.

Metaphysical abstractions confessedly mysterious, utterly contradictory, absurd, and unintelligible—deductions from half-deciphered remains of the nursery legends of the Social Organism's infancy, are jumbled up with that most insinuative deception, that immaculate abortion, the theo-morality illusion, and presented as religion! An opaque entanglement equally transcendental, subjective, and indeterminate, is consequently palmed off as law! And a treachery so inimitable as to appear, to the simple-minded, to have a direct, undeviating meaning, whilst it is susceptible of any tortuosity of construction that corrupted judges choose to give it, is, in countries where that liberty-mockery, that wildest of Utopianism, the caucus-and-ballot-box delusion, prevails, imposed as a " *Constitution!*"

The *full* operation of this subjective, transcendental, theo political hodge-podge, this consummation of religio-governmental abuse, is to give half a breakfast to the many, and half a million or so to the grasping few; con-

---

* See " Essence of Science," pages 5 to 7.
† See " Positive Philosophy," page 402.

ditioned on such vexatious anxiety on the part of the latter, lest they be added to the naked, houseless, starving multitude, by falling stocks, breaking banks, defalcations, failures, etc., etc., etc., before dinner-time, that dyspepsia, rather than nutrition, waits on what little appetite they have.

At periodical crises, these "institutions" torment so excruciatingly that even the war-horror affords relief; and bankruptcy-panics occur in such quick succession as to leave *no* intervening *complete* respite. -

This perfect mockery of religion, law, and government, its sponsors have the audacity to gravely assure mankind is civilization — enlightenment, even! And they blasphemously pronounce the extrication of man *as* man from his misery, or even the *radically* and *effectually* bettering of his *sensible* condition, to be "impossible !" And the confiding, awe-struck, wonder-confounded, and most treacherously betrayed multitude reverently bow to their decrees, and meekly accept *their* creations as the best *knowable* manifestations of infinite wisdom, love, and power!

Theo-democratic quacks worse confound this confusion, and give piquancy to its agony, by calling on all the ignorance and chicanery which it engenders, to regulate it! Elective franchise is the most effectual screen of governmental cupidity and villainy,—the subterfuge of freedom's most dangerous assassins. That medicine-chest of political quackery ; that insidious and most fatal decoy of the uncritical, short-sighted multitude—the ballot-box, is the great reservoir of the social quack-nostrums which worse and worse aggravate whatever evils they are applied to cure, till the dupes and victims of them gladly resign themselves to the comparatively tender mercies of military dictatorship.*

---

* " The only disease that afflicts either the Social Organism or individual man, is ignorance. Ignorance, with respect to the perfection of which nature, through development, including science and art, is capable. The political symptom of this disease is repression. Moral quacks, to hide their ignorance with respect to how to satisfy the human passions, gravely pronounce these passions natural depravities, and accordingly declare war against them. Repression *quickly* touches that point in agony which renders humanity frantic, in that form of government under which brute force, or majority power, managed and directed by the basest and most ignorant (except in mere trickery) of mankind, ruthlessly and *continually* trample down the most important and evident human rights (passional rights), except bare life ; *often* does not spare even that; and, equally with that more chronic human scourge—monarchy— sets aside all that can properly be called law. ' Popular Sovereignty ' is the bitterest mockery that mankind were ever insulted with. ' Elective Franchise ' is the most successful juggle, whereby political tricksters cheat a nation of its liberty, and swindle it of its wealth. The people are the mere cards

And cynics attempt to smother their consciousness of ignorance, and to hide their misanthropy, by inculcating the belief that the social compact is *inevitable* tyranny—that government is a "*necessary* evil?" What an infernal confession of faith!

But the most inconsistent *rôle* in this miserable drama is performed by those who, whilst fancying themselves fully emancipated from superstition, embrace, for their creed, that most supernatural of supernaturalisms, the morality phantasm; and proclaim, for their principal canon, that essence of the crucifixion-scheme of salvation—self-denial, or duty; who depend, for all the reform that they can conceive to be *practical*, on that pliant convertibility to even theological sophistry—reason; whose maximum of liberty, those indispensable aids to metaphysics and transcendentalism—free *thought*, and free *discussion* are to compose; and whose measure of human rights is contracted to so much comfort as individuals could secure, each for themselves, if absolutely emancipated from religion, and completely "let alone" by government; in short, if there was *no* Social Organism. These doubly-deceived victims of the most wily form of theo-religion (a form so treacherous as to exhibit *primâ facie* evidence of being earthly to skeptics, and *satisfactory* evidence of being divine to believers) try to patch up matters so as to make our social purgatory endurable, by means of promiscuous, undigested, *practically* aimless debates, and by hurling *merely negative* arguments, and carefully unsystemized and therefore barren facts and truisms at mankind indiscriminately; but mainly at those who compose the masses—the *body* of the Social Organism; and who, in accordance with materiality's orderly economy, *naturally loathe nothing so thoroughly as disquisitions on what is too general, abstract, and complicated for them to perceive its practical bearing.*

· Folly is rampant, corruption is at its height, anarchy is as triumphant as it can be. The barbarous and even savage portions of mankind persistently remain as they are, as civilization *practically* manifests only that which excites their disgust—their contempt, even.

which these gamblers shuffle at their pleasure in the great game of State. All the 'franchise' that 'election' secures, is enjoyed by those who compose the 'caucus,' do the 'wire-pulling,' and other party meanness, and *win the offices.* The people's choice is only between this or that gang of conspirators against mankind, who shriek liberty exactly in proportion as they mean oppression and spoils. The only true religion must be the science of sciences; the only free government, the art of arts."—*Essence of Science.*

Labor, capital, and skill are so antagonistically related that their interests are as insecure as they can be. There is the least possible responsibility everywhere, from the responsibility of the national treasury and national credit, to that of the most petty shop-keeper. In short, progress has yet done little more *practically* in the way of increasing the gross sum of human happiness, than the numerous arti- sans engaged in clock and watch manufacturing have done toward making time-keepers, *up to* the point where they put their wheels, springs, etc., etc., etc., together, fit their keys, and wind up.

Is there nothing further to be expected? Is nature's power taxed to the utmost? Has materiality pushed development to its goal only to cap the climax of all imagin- able absurdity? only to create man necessarily self-misled, self-cheated or cheating, and all but unendurably self- tormented? Is all that is knowable an irremediable failure?

No. I shall demonstrate that there is an intelligible, practicable, and ample cure, a scientific, artistic, *substantial* remedy for all the evil laid to the charge of nature, but which ignorance, and its resulting nonsense-religion, quack- government, and morality-delusion are inflicting on our false priest-ridden, skeptic-befooled, morality-crazed, mon- archy-crushed, aristocracy-trampled, demagogue-swindled world.

## § 6. RELIGIO-POLITICAL AXIOMS.

Religion, however true or false it may, owing to man's ignorance or knowledge, seem, must unavoidably be the *general social law* to which all others must be referable and subordinate—the theory, to which human government must be the practice. Religion is as necessary to, and inseparable from the Social *Organism*, as gravitation is necessary to, and inseparable from, the Universe. Religion is, to social law, what gravitation is to all law. Mystery revelation is self-contradictory, self-evident absurdity. Materiality is all-sufficient. Or, if it is not adequate to all the *real*, the *intelligible* demands of even the *religious* instinct, all the *knowable* is failure, and *all* is the most pitiable inefficiency, unless *nothing* is the basis of *all*, and supernaturalism is alone true.

The *significancy* of "miracle" is development; all beyond which is delusion. Perfect and "*eternal*" happiness *really* means the perfect and sufficiently lasting happiness which by science, art, and lower material aid, is producible. All the human and lower material forces developed, harmonized, modified, to their utmost capacity, and as advantageously as possible *combined*, will realize Heaven on Earth ; any shorter or lower aim than which can never reach nature's mark.

The Church, though variously named, scandalized to the last degree by the most abominable abuse, and seemingly not only fractured, but even in the last stages of decay, is founded as securely as is gravitation, and indivisibly and irrepressibly includes all mankind. Collective man is a State objectively and practically, and a Church subjectively and theoretically ; and all opposition to this relationship can but augment the evils charged to it, but which are wholly owing to ignorance with respect to its law. The head of the scientific Church will be to the State what the Sun is to the Solar System—a liberty insuring *hierarch.*

The truth of religion admits of no extraneous evidence ; *actual* and *complete* human freedom, or a rapidly increasing tendency thereunto, alone can manifest it. A Church indisputably infallible can be no other than a State throughout which liberty is *real, universal*, and *perfect*, or self-evidently and very rapidly becoming so.

The theory that all things came of nothing is treated with respect by nearly all mankind. The theory that all mankind came from one stock, and that all the geological changes which the Earth presents have taken place within the period of about six thousand years, is seriously entertained by those claiming to be eminent in science and art, and is listened to with patience even by those who dissent from it.

There has already been such enormous quantities of nothing said on the nothing theory, that I shall add no more nothing to it. But I hope those who believe in human perfection through a power they call " God," and concerning which, or whom, they confess that they *know nothing*, will candidly listen to some of the arguments, and a very few of the facts that I have glanced at and shall adduce from *a world full of them*, to show that physical perfection and human fulfillment is attainable through intelligible, substantial means—through the only power that there can be anything known, thought, or even *imagined* about, and that man can, much better than he ever has done, direct, and much more rapidly than he ever has done, accelerate the process.

And will those who have written, or carefully read large

volumes going to show that the coal-black, woolly-headed, flat-nosed, blubber-lipped, retreating-foreheaded, long-heeled Negro, the still further removed from the Caucasian race Hottentot, and the scarce human Esquimaux, came, *through natural transformations*, from the same stock as Washington and Auguste Comte, Mary Wollstonecraft and the Empress Eugenia, as have also the myriads of children who have died aged one hour, and the man who has lived one hundred and sixty-nine years, give ear and brain to the theory, which does not draw a whit more on the *amount* of nature's modifiability, that development can be carried to the extent of producing a *variety* of races [Darwin has fully demonstrated that races are not immutable] of *human* beings, all of whom shall be as beautiful, as healthy, and every way as perfect, as angels are imagined to be; and that the earth is capable of being fitted up for the perfect accommodation of such beings, and for their sustentation in life *ad libitum* as to individuals, and *eternal* as a Social Organism or Universal Man? And in view of the conquests over obstacles to his ends that man has already achieved, who that is endowed with any considerable degree of intellectual generalization can doubt that man will, with rapidly increasing speed, push perfection to its goal?

I will here remark, that the races, into which natural historians divide mankind, like the simple material elements into which physicists resolve matter, are indispensable landmarks in science and art, though it should never be lost sight of that the former are not immutable, nor are the latter ultimate; they are merely the analyses beyond which science and art *have not yet gone*.

It is in evidence that human life, in spite of all the foes that beset it, has increased in length even within the historic period, as has also the human stature. One hundred and seventy-two years have been achieved, and, in numerous instances, one hundred to one hundred and twenty. "Life," says Bichat, "is the aggregate of functions that resist death." Of course, then, all that strengthens the organs of these functions prolongs life, all that weakens them and counteracts the instinctive efforts of the *vis medicatrix naturæ* hastens death, and all that *prevents* the life organs from any advantage that they are capable of profiting by, transmits a *weaker than necessary* life-power, and a *proportionally shorter life* to posterity, and *vice versâ*. This being the case, is it not downright stupidity to say that when all the foes to life are as far overcome as possible, life will not be lengthened to any desirable extent ?

Care, vexation, ennui, and unsatisfied longing or passional starvation, cause an incalculable amount of wear and tear of the brain and nervous system.

The malarious effluvia that floats in the atmosphere, that has, in many localities, been greatly reduced by human means, attended with a corresponding lengthening of life, and that is wholly removable, still causes, *everywhere*, an immense wear and tear on all the organs of life, particularly the liver, lungs, and, sympathetically, the heart.

The death-power that lurks in the best food or drinks *now* obtainable, except, *in some rare instances*, water, wears out the stomach and intestines fearfully in advance.

The ignorance that prevails with respect to ventilating and heating houses, temples, theatres, lecture-rooms, and public conveyances, actually gouges the lungs prematurely to pieces.

If physiologists were not, like physicists, wholly absorbed in scientific *specialities*, how could they *not* perceive that the ossification of the arteries that impedes the free circula- tion of blood in the parts—do. of the cartilages that dimin- ishes the capillary system of the lungs and prevents sangui- fication, can be retarded by diet and other means, as can also the shrivelling and induration of the nervous system which renders it unfit for innervation ?—particularly after we have learned more of the nature of life, which physiologists are so assiduously striving to do ?

Sydenham admits that two-thirds of mankind die of acute diseases, two-ninths of consumption, and one-ninth from other chronic maladies, and from old age. How strange it is that it did not occur to him that none of the co-sharers of the morbidity that he admits all to have passed the ordeal of, could possibly die of anything at all deserving the name of old age. But few men of special science are capable of drawing general conclusions.

## § 7. RELIGIO-POLITICAL THEOREMS.

Nature—all in man's connection—all the humanly per- ceptible, is spontaneously changing to an organism through- out which complete harmony and all conceivable perfection will reign. For her means are adequate to her ends ; she has not, even through human thought, gone out of herself ; subjectivity cannot transcend objectivity.

In the animal kingdom, nature has attained to consciousness ; man is her cerebrum, the lower animals her cerebel-
lum.   All mind, thought, or will is, in the broadest or most
general sense, the mind, thought, or will, of entire nature—
of all which to man exists.

Specially considered, the mind, or soul, whether of man
or of lower animals, is the function of cerebral organism
*positively*, and of all or any part of external and cognizable
nature, *negatively*.

### § 8.  TRUE RELIGION THE SCIENCE OF SCIENCES.

Man's highest aspiration—his religious instinct—his
fancied supernatural yearning, is the manifestation of
nature's self-tendency to that perfection which she is ela-
borating.   All that man hopes for from " miracle," he will
*substantially obtain* through science, art, and lower material development.

Instinctively, during savageism, barbarism, and civilism,
man fancifully abstracts his subjectivity, and as fancifully
creates it almighty ; and this anthropomorphitic or " theologic " phantasm foreshadows, and really signifies the
almightiness to which man will, *objectively*, arrive.   Triune
matter, motion,* and mind, is rapidly throwing off its mystical envelope—the triune " Father, Son, and Holy Ghost."
Man has already eliminated supernatural divinity from, and
manifested his own divinity in, a great portion of nature.
He is *acknowledged* lord of the materiality of which all is
composed, to the extent to which the air-balloon, the steam-
engine, the electro-magnetic telegraph, and their accompanying sciences and arts manifest ; and as soon as he thoroughly understands that *he is God*—when God-incarnation
stands a known reality, instead of an inexplicable, sense-
confounding, malice-breeding, improvement-hindering " mystery," God-man will rapidly direct all the force which produces evil, to the production of good ; and (with a velocity
increasing as do numbers successively multiplied by their
own products) complete the process of making all existence
in his connection as conducive to his happiness as it was
inimical to it when human progress was at its lowest stage.
Development and art near completion—human and lower

---

* I have herein before called *Man* the second person in the *intelligible* Trinity, but lest this should be considered a self-contradiction, I will remark, that
Man is the most important manifestation of nature's motion, and the exponent
of her dynamics.

material perfection—with a power of means increasing as
the speed with which the celestial spheroids, if thrown into
confusion, would gravitate to equilibrium. For the Social
Organism is as susceptible of *order and freedom* as that
planetary empire whose chief is the Sun has proved to be;
and the *Universal Organism* harmonized to the extent that
it is self-capable of being, and thus self-enabled to bring all
its force to bear for good, will clear up the immortality
enigma, and solve the liberty problem.

Without the aid of miracle, but by human and lower
material means, all existence in the human connection will
be one grand laboratory of good; the Earth will be so
equally inhabitable as to form but an *agreeable* variety of
climate, from the equator to the poles, leaving no nook for
savageism, ignorance and superstition to skulk in; and there
will be, between desiring and having, only the intervention
of just exertion enough to give due value to possession; and
human life will be extended till all the varieties of happiness presentable to the five senses exhaust their value by
repetition.

After making all possible allowance for the diversity of
temperature, which ocean and air currents cause, there
remains an approximation of the temperature of the warmest
days in winter to that of the coldest days in summer, and a
difference in the mean temperature (seven degrees in the
*inland* city of St. Louis) of *whole years*, utterly incompatible with the theory that the sun, or the inclination of
the earth's axis toward the plane of its equator, inducing
obliquity of radiation, cause what are vulgarly called "heat"
and "cold," to any *excess* that may not be reduced to perfect geniality by human means, acting in concert with
lower material ones.

Every one knows that some earthly bodies are self-lumi-
nous; and it is in evidence that the planets do not borrow
all their light from the sun. The *Aurora Borealis* is very
significant of a powerful means whereby, when electrical,
thermal and luminous action are better understood, "light"
will be sufficiently extended to the earth's poles. The
extraordinary lightness of some whole nights in particular
places *far removed from polar twilight* (see Humboldt's
remarks thereon) is wholly unaccountable in the *present*
knowledge of the crepuscular theory, and shows conclusively
that luminosity may be generated to an extent not yet
dreamed of, in our atmosphere, or that the latter, being
modifiable even *spontaneously*, so as to reflect brightness from

the sun, to the extent that fine print can be read at midnight *even near the equator*, will prove sufficiently modifiable for all human purposes.

Let any one with a capacity for drawing comprehensive deductions, take into consideration the remarkable phenomena noted by Dr. Kane during his Arctic Explorations, and see if they do not immeasurably more sustain the theory herein set forth, than they do the wretchedly barren one, that the world is such an unfinished and unfinishable piece of botchery, that it is a mere kennel to breed mutually tormenting knaves and fools in, or "a fleeting show for man's illusion given," in which to make some mystical preparations for enjoying life in a world so utterly unintelligible that we can *know nothing at all about it !* A world which, the God of this present one, in order to mend his hand at creation, and not *utterly* disgrace himself in the estimation of his creatures, has prepared for them to be happy in, *after they are dead !*

The wide range north and south, which isothermal lines take in their progress east and west, and which is as yet only partially accounted for, is encouragingly significant. The curves which these lines take in passing all the highest polar latitudes yet reached by navigators, indicate the existence of a warmer clime in the open sea or vast plains at the flattened poles.

## § 9. RIGHT GOVERNMENT THE ART OF ARTS.

The conditions for all desirable good *can* and *must* be produced. Whatever aims to repress, instead of to satisfy, the natural passions, is either folly, quackery, or fraud. Civil law can no more be "enacted" than physical law can. It must be discovered. Let that figment of the imagination—duty, and its horrid correlate—the evil-for-evil delusion, be consigned to where science and art have doomed so many less complicated barbarisms. Let moral government, arrogant government, and caucus-and-ballot-box government—those abortive and utopian experiments, which are now self-evident failures, together with those bewildering barrennesses—metaphysics and skepticism, be buried in the same grave with their long since defunct parent, supernaturalism; and let man avail himself of nature's ample resources, and go scientifically and artistically to work to make himself *really* good, *perfectly* happy, in short, *actually* free. Let man set about the inauguration of Heaven on Earth as dispassionately and determinedly, and in as *good* and *real faith* as he combines labor, capital and skill to construct railroads, factories, and steamships, and complete success will crown his efforts.

## § 10. HOW TRUE RELIGION AND RIGHT GOVERNMENT WILL COMMENCE TO BE ESTABLISHED.

In proportion as the clergy understand the gospel of development, science and art, they will expand the budding organs* of the human understanding, and rightly direct, instead of mystery-confounding man's religious instinct. As religion thus becomes emancipated from its primitive savage and barbarous miracle-absurdity, and stands revealed the science of sciences, government must necessarily correspond to it, by changing from that abomination of abominations now submitted to as "*necessary evil*," to the art of arts whereby perfection will be *realized*.

Or, if the present *mockery* of a clergy continue deaf to the demands of the age, and blind to the highest interests both of themselves and the rest of mankind (for I think I have made it apparent that until *all* have their rights, *no one* can have them), the hour is surely and rapidly approaching when they will be displaced by a *true* priesthood, who will, in temples far more splendid than any hitherto built, and as much better furnished as the practical and sufficient is preferable to the speculative and impossible—as meaning is superior to balderdash, give mankind *real, body-and mind-satisfying* truth, in place of bewildering, *sense and-passion-opposing* fallacy—the kernel, instead of the swine's fodder of husks, with which they are now fed.

Half the money that Stephen Girard so vainly and blindly devoted to *indiscriminately opposing religion*, would be sufficient to found a church that would form the nucleus of the universal one that will divest religion of savage mystery and vindictiveness, and enable it to stand *revealed* the re-

---

* *The* clergy always have been, and *a* clergy necessarily must be, the *real* governors of mankind. "Let me make the people's songs," said Napoleon I., "and I care not who make their laws." And it is to me perfectly astonishing that the meanest capacity does not comprehend that emperors, kings, presidents, parliaments, Congresses, etc. etc., are but the subalterns—the very tools of those who make the people's cradle-hymns and Sunday-school catechisms : that "infidels" do not perceive where their *only* remedy against superstition lies, and that the miserable demagogues do not understand that so long as the clergy stick to "Christ and him crucified," as they are so anxious to have them do, they, the demagogues, will have to travel the same mean, contemptible, hard, *never* safe, and *usually* fatal road they now do.

splendent combination of all science; would be sufficient
to found and permanently establish as the foundation-stone
of the basis of the eternal well-being of the Social Organism,
a church, under the guidance of which, physical training
and object-teaching, *adapted to the varying human capacities*,
would displace mystery, metaphysics, moralism, in short,
vindictive, subjective teaching; a church in which music,
painting, eloquence, poetry, sculpture—all that can attract,
physically and mentally develop and socialize mankind—all
that can charm woman, enlist her mighty influence, emancipate her, and render her, without exception, so adorable,
that love will be universally reciprocal between her and
commensurately developed man; all that can *amuse* and
*suitably* instruct without *boring* the masses; all that can
qualify for man's leaders those whom nature has formed for
such—formed to be the Social Organism's head.   A church
in which what is capable of producing all this—all conceivable perfection—would be *used* instead of *abused*.

More than on anything else, human emancipation depends
on woman finding her right position in the Social Organism.
The time has already arrived for commencing the *practical*
solution of this question.  *Progress waits on it.*  If man
exceeds woman in strength of body, and has a more substantial mental organization, she possesses an enchanting
physical loveliness, and a superiority with respect to certain
intellectual qualities, to which he is indebted for his most
vivid sensations of delight.   This renders her to him, what
the blossoms and foliage of the tree are to the body and
roots thereof.   Woman is *more* than man's equal, so sure as
the being that he spontaneously, *really*, and *necessarily*
*adores*, is above him; and she will be far more than at
present, the object of man's adoration, when humanity is
perfected.  Between unsophisticated lovers, the very acme
of delight is spontaneous adoration on the part of the man,
and the reception of it on that of the woman; and the
adored must be considered superior to the adorer, when adoration is spontaneous, and *delightfully accorded*, rather than
when it is extorted by fear.  If man ungallantly tells woman
that—"the beautiful could not exist, but for the substantial," she can truly retort, and generally with an air that
will bow him ecstatic at her feet, "but the substantial
would soon wish itself out of existence were it not for the
beautiful."  Woman's rights can never be secured by her
competing with man *in his sphere*.  If he yields, she will be
only the pitiable recipient of charity.  If he competes with

*all* his force, her rights will be far more brutally trampled on than they now are.

Are not *exceedingly* beautiful women *deified* even now? and are not woman's rights very perceptibly more secure in proportion to woman's physical and intellectual beauty? A beautiful woman enters a crowded car. All the men rise, as if magically operated upon, to give her a seat. A rather ugly one enters. If she is not so old as to excite pity, she will stand some time before *any one* will offer her a chance to sit down. Develop the physical, and the moral will take care of itself. In the coquetry which shallow philosophers and blindly stupid moralists sneer at, there is a most important, and, in the economy of nature, a most valuable reality.

Of course, the members of the *true* Church could neither be hoaxed into voting—into being the mere chess-men of political gamblers, nor fooled into law-suits. They would settle their own differences among themselves, or by an appeal to their religio-governmental dignitaries, who would *know* that their own interests were as inseparable from those of their fellow-citizens, as the interests of the head are from those of the body. They would avoid differences with the rest of the world as much as possible, and in *no* emergency condescend to enter their inextricably perplexing arena—"law." Pending the existence of laws *against* collecting debts (for that is *exactly* what *all* laws ostensibly *for* collecting debts amount to), they would stick as close to the cash system of trade as possible.

As this *practically* good, and *really* free Church and State organization enlarged its area and extended its operations, it would *harmoniously regulate*, instead of *arbitrarily* governing, *every thing;* agriculture, manufactures, commerce—all. In architecture, man would have the advantage of chemical and biological science with respect to ventilation. In the matter of clothing, the tailor and dress-maker, and especially their customers, would have the inestimable advantage derivable from the knowledge of the physician. The hygienic department would also see that grain was harvested and fruit gathered, and cookery done, immeasurably more to the advantage of health and longevity than they now are. Quack liberty ignores science in the social economy, or else commits the equal folly of supposing that every individual can master all science. The bogus *constitutional* and sham *legal freedom* of the members of the body politic to murder the whole community by poison, suffocation, strangulation, and a thousand other means, would be wholly disallowed, to their own inestimable advantage.

When the power of this freedom-dispensing hierarchy arrived at the requisite point, all children born would have the advantage of all the physical and intellectual culture that the organization to which they belonged could give them. They would be *wholly at the charge of the State.* No reason can be urged against this, that is not equally valid against our present public schools, and no reason can be given against an universal joint-stock equitable arrangement of the interests of labor, skill, capital, and *all human concerns*, that is not valid against public libraries, public roads, the public defence, and, in short, against everything that *generally accommodates.*

The first governmental *public* accommodation, was the irrepressible movement toward a universal copartnership that will *really* emancipate labor, *sufficiently* remunerate skill, and *perfectly* secure capital; in short, enable individuals to exist in society as freely as the planets revolve in the solar system; so free, that between wishing and having there will intervene but just exertion enough to give due value to possession.

The founding of a church like the one above sketched will be the beginning of the end of anarchy, oppression, and wrong. Superstition will thenceforth be rapidly curtailed, and good, instead of evil, will as rapidly become spontaneous.

The first church that successfully commences this great revolution, will be the nucleus of the Sun of the religio-governmental system that will include the world itself, both physical and human. It will include all mankind, and all in the human connection: all which acts on man, and is therefore, positively or negatively, acted on by man.

The Cathedral that is in contemplation for Bishop Hughes, or the mammoth meeting-house that is in prospect for the Rev. Henry Ward Beecher, backed by the wealth of a few millionaires, and the official aid of the eminent men of science and the artists that wait but a call from such a corporation, would probably be successful. At any rate, it would be immeasurably more glorious to take the first step in this enterprise that is perfectly sure to succeed eventually, though it should, *pro tempore*, fail, than it would be to be Emperor or President of the world, under present circumstances. Oh, how pitiably contemptible the mightiest theologically constituted monarchs and demagogues will appear, and how abominably the names of our most bunkum theo-democratic politicians will stink, when man's good opinion is worth having—when what we now call man *is* man.

What powerful capitalists—what influential clergymen—what eminent scientists and artists will take the lead in this supremely magnificent revolution (this revolution of revolutions, that will crown and fructify all former ones), and thus gain the inestimable satisfaction of inaugurating Heaven on Earth, secure to their names the *gloria in excelsis* of all future ages, and embalm their memories in the grateful affections of *Eternal Man?* Of man, when his approbation shall be an honor ; when he shall be as free, as happy, as wise, and as perfect, as the author of "The Religion of Science" thus prophetically pictures him :

"The scene of my vision now rapidly shifted from stage to stage of development and progress, till it reached the thirtieth century ;* the substantial glory and magnificence of each succeeding stage, increasing in the ratio (in which science and art within our own observation does) of the multiplication of numbers by each succeeding product ; till, finally, the ice in the Polar regions disappeared, the superfluous thermal activity in the Equatorial regions was suitably diminished, and luminous action was sufficient everywhere. Sciences on Sciences and Arts on Arts had, working with, or according to, nature, fully developed her, liberated all her laws, and availed *perfectly organized* Man of *the use of all her force most advantageously combined.*

"The whole earth was cultivated in a manner far superior to that in which any portion of it now is. Magnificent palaces, about six miles apart, had displaced all the isolated abodes of jealousy, vexation, misery and ennui. Children were no longer dreaded as a burden by either parent, and were hailed as precious and valuable acquisitions by the State, which not only provided for their perfect development as members of it, but honored and remunerated mothers for their bearing and suckling, by an equivalent for the loss of time to which they were thereby subjected. This remuneration did not consist in silver or gold dollars—the coinage of barbarism ; nor in all but or quite worthless shin-plasters—the currency of pseudo civilization ; but in certificates of value based on actual production ; or, which amounted to the same thing, in stock, by which nearly all property was represented. All mankind composed one vast joint stock corporation.

"Prostitution, either for life, for a single night, or by the job, was of course banished. Volcanoes were silenced, tempests were hushed, pestilence and disease had ceased, and the earth's circulations were as genial as were those of the perfectly healthy human body, which had at last been realized.

"Nearly all labor was done by machinery. The balmy air was navigated by gorgeous balloons. No clothing, except for ornament, was necessary, and none other was worn. The women, released by religio-governmental science and art; and by enlightened public opinion, from every inconvenience connected with free maternity, were all more en-

* Common Era.

chantingly beautiful than the Houris with which even Asiatic imagination has furnished Mahomet's Paradise; they were very Goddesses, revelling most voluptuously in the adoration which the equally faultless men as voluptuously yielded them. Lovers (and *all* were such) freely, spontaneously, and harmlessly luxuriated in each other's embraces.

"All were equally beautiful without being alike; so that the only reason for choosing one rather than another was the love of variety. The great problem of the reciprocalness of love was solved, by all being so faultless, both physically and mentally, that love was universally reciprocal. Restraint was banished, virtue was no more, and vice was obsolete.

"Throughout perceptible nature, all was perfection; desire was the measure of fulfillment; to will was to have, with the intervention of just exertion enough to give due value to possession.

"Would that I could portray, somewhat in detail, the magnificence, the luxury, the bliss, which resulted from the full triumph of the Religion and Government of Science. But our now paucity of objects of comparison prevents me. Give your imaginations the reins, ye who are most gifted in that respect; stick to *coherency*, and you cannot go astray; though the most sanguine will fall very far short of the glorious reality.

"The following is the first Lesson of *The Catechism*, which I heard the children (*real* flesh and blood angels) in a primary school reciting:

"*Question.* Wherein consists the value of all existence?

"*Answer.* In happiness.

"*Q.* To what should all human endeavor, therefore, aim?

"*A.* To the acquisition, perfection, and sufficient prolongation of happiness.

"*Q.* How do you know that happiness is *rightly* the sole object for which you should strive?

"*A.* I *feel* it to be so. I *cannot* desire anything else. Besides, there is nothing else worth aiming at, or even living for.

"*Q.* Is it right for you to strive to promote *only your own* happiness?

"*A.* It is.

"*Q.* How do you know it to be right?

"*A.* From the fact that it is impossible for me voluntarily to strive for anything else.

"*Q.* What guaranty have mankind always had, that perfect and sufficiently *lasting* happiness as to the *individual*, and perfect and *eternal* happiness as to the *species*, were attainable?

"*A.* Nature's; whose highest consciousness, and intelligence, man is. The seed, the hope, the glimmering foreknowledge, of the great harvest of happiness which we are now reaping, nature planted in man when, through development, she first rough-created him; and so deep, that it never could be uprooted, but must necessarily have come, as it now has, to *full* maturity, to complete verification, where, in virtue of nature's *law of laws*, it *must* remain, as *inexhaustible* as the *race* of man is *eternal;* as perpetual as is the equilibrium of the celestial spheroids.

"*Q.* During the age of mystery, when man was in his primitive imperfection, in his physical and therefore intellectual heterogeneity—what name did his bewildered imagination give to the object of his *individual* existence?

"*A.* *Eternal* happiness.

" *Q.* Wherein consisted his mistake?

" *A.* In not comprehending the Social Organism, or *collective* man— The *Eternal Being* to whom alone *eternal happiness* could *be happiness ;* and in not knowing that *temporal* happiness could be made to last *long enough* to be *quite sufficient* for the *temporal* beings which, through nature's law of individual change, successively constitute *eternal* Humanity.

" *Q.* How do you know that our present harvest of perfect happiness is inexhaustible, and that *our race* is fixed in eternal happiness?

" *A.* The laws of the intellectual world follow the rule of those of the physical, on which they depend; and the Social Organism is now as harmoniously, and therefore as permanently, adjusted to all in its connection as is the solar system. Man's—nature's—spontaneous yearning for satisfaction has, aided by all in the connection, produced in the world of man, that *necessarily eternal* order which answers to the *equilbrium* which gravitation has, thus aided, produced in the planetary world. The *eternal* happiness of collective man, and the perfect and sufficiently lasting happiness of *individual* man are, therefore, as assured as is the order of the celestial spheroids.

" *Q.* In what relation do you stand toward all mankind?

" *A.* All mankind, from the first inseparably, though for a long time heterogeneously connected, are now, happily, a harmoniously organized whole; of which I am a part, in as *strict* sympathy with all the other parts, as the most minute tissues of my body are in sympathy with all the rest of it.

" *Q.* It seems, then, that you cannot do an act which will promote your own happiness, without *simultaneously* doing one which *must* promote the good of all mankind; nor can you do an act fraught with evil to others, which will not *surely* redound to your own hurt. Do you comprehend all this?

" *A.* As easily as I understand that my whole body shares the sensation of dissatisfaction caused by the prick of a needle on the end of my little finger, or that of satisfaction, caused by the contact of my palate with food; or that of delight, caused by my eyes beholding, my ears hearing, and my brains understanding, the pleasure which all around me experience.

" *Q.* But though you are as *really*, you are not as *closely* connected with the rest of mankind, as the parts of your body are with yourself. How does the body politic immediately bring its all-sufficient power to bear in preventing wrong action?

" *A.* By means of that body's nerves and brain—its Scientific Discoverers and Directors. By means of these, I acquire the aid of the whole force of the body politic and of all else in the connection, and am thus enabled to shape my actions in accordance with the social organism's welfare, and simultaneously with the welfare of every part of it, necessarily including myself. My functions, like those of the *mass* of mankind, are special; those of a few, but *naturally* sufficient number, are general.

" *Q.* Are you and your compeers who compose the *mass* of mankind, then, but mere blind followers of your superiors?

" *A.* Blind? no indeed. Our *understandings*, and particularly our *feelings*, are constantly wide awake to the *results* which acting in accordance with the directions of our social functionaries produces. For the rest, we *have no superiors* in any *arbitrary* sense of the word.

2*

"*Q.* But what guaranty have you that your general function aries will not misguide you, or shape your action for their own special benefit?

"*A.* They can no more be benefited by injuring us, than my individual nerves and brain can be benefited by damaging my muscles; *and they know it.* They know that our wretchedness would necessitate their misery; that the only difference between their woes and ours would be that theirs would be gilded and ours but varnished. We, the masses, have the same guaranty that our Scientific Discoverers and Directors will not wrong us, that my hand has, that my nerves and brain will not misdirect it into the fire.

"Here the first Lesson ended; and music, instrumental and vocal, incomparably more fairy-like than any I had ever yet heard, fell on the charmed ear, and the rest of the session was spent in all that could enliven instruction and render it attractive."

## § 11. BUSINESS PANICS.

But we want something *immediately* practical; we want manufacturers "going ahead," a "smashing trade" doing, "confidence restored" to credit, money plenty, secession quieted, and the negro-question settled *right away*, clamor the short-sighted, impatient multitude.

To those who think their deepest when they talk thus, I have said nothing, and shall say nothing respecting *how* religio-governmental science and art will produce their perfectly satisfactory results. Not that I despise "The People," or entertain the slightest disrespect for their judgment, but the contrary. *I would not mock them.* Their views are (in accordance with nature's perfect economy) special; mine, the powers that have *constituted me* have made general, or more comprehensive. I honor the masses in their proper sphere; in the *only* sphere in which they have ever shown *capability to benefit themselves.* Let them extend to me the same civility, follow the prescription that I am, by the *All and in All,* constituted to give, and judge by the result. Have they not over and over tried all else sufficiently to learn that they thereby only continue the doubly deceived and betrayed dupes—the mere tools of those miserable demagogues who are making them *supremely* ridiculous, and who, equally blind and self-duped, are leading the way, deeper and deeper into the present social quagmire? Have "The People" not been long enough fooled by political quacks, whose *special* applications change but do not cure— whose *soi-disant* "practical measures" are but a miserable series of delusive experiments that shift the diseased Social Organism's position, only to make its maladies more and more chronic and the cure more complicated?

Away with such temporizing, *as fast as possible ;* social ills can no more be cured suddenly, than the most chronic bodily ills can. The public can no more bound from its present complication of the deepest seated and most chronic social maladies into *real* prosperity, than some quack-pill can instantaneously cure scrofula—than an impatient novice can jump into Greek, Latin, Arithmetic, etc., etc., without first learning the alphabet and the figures.

### § 12. WAGES-SLAVERY AND CHATTEL-SLAVERY.

The American Ship of State is in the very breakers of dissolution. The bar on which she is splitting, is the following clause in " *The* Constitution."\* " No person held to service or labor in one State, under the laws thereof, escaping into another, shall, in consequence of any law or regulation therein, be discharged from such service or labor, but shall be delivered up on claim of the party to whom such service or labor may be due."

I trust that those to whom I have been appealing have become convinced of the transitory and at best provisional nature of all hitherto religion, law, governments, and even constitutions; that " *The* Constitution " was but *the highest step in progress that America could attain to seventy-three years ago ;* that if it was for all future ages, science, art, and *all* improvements, are fallacies ; that the time is surely approaching when no one will " *owe* service or labor," either as a chattel-slave or wages-slave; or shall serve a less august master than the real, the substantial, the intelligible Almighty ; nor shall work at all except on conditions dictated by himself; conditions that will secure to himself *perfect* and *sufficiently lasting* happiness.

I have herein-before advocated the licensing and provisionally regulating of all evil, until it can be done away with ; we should thus never for a moment have lost sight of the important fact, that *society at large is the principal party to all evil or " crime,"* and the commonest capacity will be able to perceive that all government hitherto constituted is but licensed, somewhat regulated, wholesale brigandage, at

---

\* They who are breaking up " the Union," equally with those who are trying to hold it together, claim to act in accordance with that altogether too accommodating political weathercock, " *The* Constitution," and profess the most patriotic and unwavering devotion to that immaculate indefiniteness. How much longer shall mankind be mocked and betrayed by governments founded on mystery, transcendentalism, metaphysics, subjectism ; in short, unintelligibility?

length so ripe for destruction, that it ought to give way, as fast as possible, to a religio-governmental system, founded on science and art.

Let this doctrine be preached and practiced, and *let the perfection point be constantly in view*, and evil will give way through a system of gradual, but faster and faster reduction, and those most abominable of all quack methods, cauterization or excision—punishment and *bloody* and *devastating* revolution, will never more be applied.

There is no class of southern slaves, the average length of whose lives is not much greater than is that of the lives of the sewing girls, and many classes of laborers and mechanics at the North, although the Caucasian race is naturally longer lived than the African race, and has the advantage of a more congenial climate.

Licensing the African slave-trade, instead of vainly trying to prevent it, would, long ago, have rendered the human chattel system unprofitable throughout all this land, the fertility of which is not, like that of Egypt, recuperable through the overflowing of rivers; and immediately have given whole States like Missouri, and particularly Virginia, the *advantage* of a system of human slavery *much worse for the sufferers*, but which must, nevertheless, be the connecting link between chattel-slavery and an equitable adjustment of the claims of labor, skill, and capital. For the advocates of wages-slavery boast, in effect, that the deceitful, fraudulent emancipation they contend for, extorts twice as much unrequited toil as does honestly acknowledged, *undisguised* slavery. And that it extorts four or five times the ingenuity, or brain-labor, that *direct* slavery does, and is proportionally more productive, is amply proven by the fact that northern man-owners are much more wealthy than are southern ones. Keep it in mind, that man's labor constitutes all of *value* in man, that either northerners or southerners own.

Licensing the slave-trade would have put a great damper on Caucasian and African amalgamation, that fruitful source of insurrection, and would rapidly have abolished the breeding of chattel-slaves in some States to supply a market in others, and the accompanying cruelty of separating children from chattel-slave parents much more sensitive than are wild Africans. I say *chattel-slave parents*, that the reader may not forget that wages-slavery also most heart-rendingly separates parents from children, and wives from husbands, and as often, too, probably, as does chattel-slavery. I have spent a year amidst "the institution" of the South, and must confess that my feelings were never *more* wounded there, by the sight of family separations at the auction-block, than they have been often and again at the steamboat landings in New York, when emigrants from the east were, *by necessity as stern as the last blow of an auctioneer's hammer,* compelled to separate, parents from children, brothers and sisters from each other, and wives from husbands, amidst sobs as audible and sighs as deep as any I had ever heard in or about the "slave-pens."

But the great difficulty is the way of licensing African importation was the opposition of the *government* of England; and, apropos of *its* objecting to slavery in *any* form, unless it directs its attention with respect to it straight homeward, the reader is requested to turn these leaves backward, and read a note on page 7.

The white slave-owners of England and our northern States pay a round license for their most artfully disguised piracy, that supports alms-houses wherein more human woe exists than would, in all probability, on board *regulated* slave-ships. Read Oliver Twist, and visit our "poor-houses," and form your judgments in the case.

If it can be shown that Protestantism is the height of religious reform, that human liberation can never proceed beyond "infidelity," demagoguocracy, and wages-slavery, let such names as Huss, Luther, Rousseau, Paine, Washington, Lafayette, Fourier, and Auguste Comte, be consigned to eternal infamy, and let *all* emancipationists be suppressed as miscreants who are wantonly disturbing—well, I had like to have said—*the peace!*

But if, on the contrary, it has been, (as I claim it has by myself, aided by those who have studied this vast subject before me,) shown that perfect human liberation is practical, then, every clause in " *The* Constitution," and every "enacted" law has got to succumb to the fate that has already befell so many kindred barbarisms; and it is as useless to contend against this, as it would be to make decrees to stop gravitation.

In view of this let us go lovingly, calmly, *scientifically,* and *artistically* to work to displace evil by good, and we shall, more and more rapidly, and, at last, with a suddenness and ease that will make every one wonder why it had not been done ages before, establish Heaven on Earth.

To talk about its being wrong for man to own property in man, is the most drivelling twaddle—the most short-sighted imbecility. Man never owned any other property and never can. Is the *negro*, or his *labor*, that which constitutes *all* the value of ownership? Evidently, the white laborer of the North and the black laborer of the South are equally owned; the latter, by a master who has an *immediate* interest in providing for his grosser necessities, the former by a master who has not even that poor incentive in his favor. The whole question evidently is, to make man's property in man mutually and universally beneficent.

If our southern States shall be so tyrannized over by a wretched mob, led on by bankrupt demagogues, and disappointed and therefore desperate politicians, as to dissolve the Union, chattel-slavery will come to the same crisis that wages-slavery is in the throes of in continental Europe, is on the very eve of in England, and is fast verging to in our northern States; not to cure, but only to render the horrible disease more chronic, and the cure more complicated.

But *machinery* is fast bringing to a *final* crisis both wages-slavery and chattel-slavery, as is manifest by the vast amount of human *muscle* it throws into armies, filibustering expeditions, alms-houses, and itinerant mendicancy; and by the multitudes of females it is plunging into the maelstrom of prostitution.

I know, indeed, that political economists deceive themselves and their readers into the idea that machinery works as well for the poor as for the rich, by making the necessaries of life more accessible; but the more and more rapid growth of the abominations I have just alluded to, flatly belies their theory. With the exception of those who are employed in making and tending machinery, what but loss and ruin does the laborer derive from it? Take the number of the unemployed, including paupers, and of the employed, and average the amount of their labor. Retrace history one hundred years, or even fifty, and do the same; and see if the average *muscle-power* exerted now, produces anything like the amount of human comforts it did then.

And they who do not calculate that machinery will, before long, make the power of even chattel-enslaved muscle unprofitable even in the bottom-lands of America, are very blind, or else I am. It would not be stranger than was the discovery of the electro-magnetic telegraph and the sewing-machine, if some cute Yankee should do that identical thing some clear morning before breakfast.

"Well, even in that case," methinks I hear too many

Patriarchs exclaim, "we shall want our negroes for waiters and body-servants." Nay, gentlemen, the attainment of the stage in progress just alluded to, will necessitate a reconstruction of society so thorough, that, if you have never studied the subject before, were I to describe it, you would think yourselves reading a new chapter in the "*Arabian Nights*," instead of a strictly scientific, though prospective portrayal.

Gentlemen, the isolated abodes of *false* selfishness, jealousy, ennui, discontent; in short, misery, both North and south, will, at the stage of progress just alluded to, rapidly give place to *palaces of delight*, as magnificent as imagination can paint; in which, breakfasts, dinners, suppers, lodgings, clean linen, and elegant apparel, will, without either slaves or servants, be furnished, unattended by the blows, scolding, and disappointment that now accompany our present wretched mockery of both comforts and pleasures.

And what is to be done with this great question of machinery against muscle? Is it not high time to have done with blinking it? To what point in beggary and starvation do those who, as capitalists and discoverers or "inventors" own machinery, expect that they who make and tend it will, even as quietly as they now do, reduce themselves?

The unemployed muscle of Europe is now in imminent battle-array, and the clouds that hang so ominously over our own political horizon, are, in sober fact, charged with the thunder of the labor question, that can never be settled short of an adjustment that will give all a share in what little labor will need to be done, and an equitable amount of the profits which such labor, in connection with the skill and capital that it will make profitable, will produce.

If the strife between the money-barons and their serfs ever comes to blows in good earnest, the battle will be far bloodier than was that between the feudal barons and their serfs. But *no*. Continental Europe is not going to be given up to red republicanism, England to levelling chartism, our northern States to starvation's saturnalia, nor our southern States to Africanization. Nineteenth century advancement has vetoed all this. Besides, Europe, and particularly France, will never forget the crushing she had under the wheels of the car of equality during the Revolution of 1789; the pitiless crushings of the wheels of that dread car have, through modern European history, exerted a salutary influence in our northern States, and the massacres of Hayti will still significantly and healthfully warn our southern brethren, some ugly looking appearances to the contrary notwithstanding.

That the Negro race, and all inferior races will run out, is at length demonstrated. In fact, the Caucasian race itself will be completely transformed. The succeeding transcendently superior races of human beings will be precisely all that the most lively *coherent* imagination can desire : and different from, without being, in the main, inferior to each other.

In order to prevent a violent crisis of wages-slavery, and gradually and peaceably end that abomination, there must be adopted measures as different from alms-giving, as productive industry is different from industrious mendicancy ; soup-committees, alms-houses, and street-charities but augment the evil they so blindly try to cure.

And in order that chattel-slavery may die out peaceably, the States wherein it exists must turn their attention, not to the prevention and reclamation of runaways, but to the best method of getting *seasonably*, *quietly* and *effectually* rid of their discontented slaves, especially if they happen to be mulattoes.

Mulattoes are as much more than *half* Caucasian, as the Caucasian blood is superior to that of the African ; and to argue that they can be enslaved, either by the lash-smart or the starvation-spur, either individually or nationally, without danger, is to ignore the battle of Bunker Hill, and deny that there ever was such a thing as rebellion, signalized by carnage and devastation.

Where the African race has been crossed by the Caucasian, slavery, of whatever kind, is evidently most degrading to the latter ; and they who think that white blood can be enslaved without danger of insurrection, by mingling it with black blood, have simply studied natural history backward, provided that they ever examined the subject at all, except with the eyes of that narrow, gross, *false* self-regard, that is the sure precursor of self-destruction.

During ten years past, the slave-rendition clause in "The Constitution" has been enforced only in that mock-sense in which "the Sabbath" has been kept sacred by the noisy disturbance necessary to a police descent on social and peaceable dancers, theatre-goers and actors, and lager beer tasters. It is safe to calculate—in fact, the advocates of the eternal fulfillment of the slave clause acknowledge—that every slave returned in accordance with it, has cost his owner, on the average, three times his value, and the government from five to ten times that amount; ignoring, for the sake of the main argument, how much less than nothing all slaves who, of their own accord run away, are really worth.

If some *practical* disposition was made of the rendition clause in " *The* Constitution," a contract, providing for the rendition of those, whether white or black, who were fugitives from States where they had been stirring up, or trying to stir up, insurrection, could unquestionably be rigidly enforced, as long as there would be any occasion for so doing. Come, brothers, let's not take leave of our rationality; for 'twill be as vain and unprofitable to break limbs, scatter brains, and let out bowels over this affair, as it was for Paddy to insist that the captain who had agreed to " take him over the sa " should " stick to his bargain," even if the ship did sink.

Nothing is plainer, than that, throughout nature, the weaker must succumb to the stronger; and this *necessarily* involves neither tyranny, oppression, nor injustice, but the very reverse. What could be more oppressive, tyrannical or unjust, than for the inferior to rule, or even be admitted to equality (if such a scheme can be even imagined in practice) with the superior? Under such a regime, how long would it be before all that was either beautiful or utile in nature would be extinguished, and this prospectively fair world of ours be reduced to a disgusting muck heap?

Until we look to entire reorganization in religion and government, every sect and party will, and with truth, scornfully toss at every other one the barren truism—*we are no worse than you are;* and the advocates of chattel ownership of human beings, and those of the wages ownership of them, will continue, and with equal justice and spite, to hurl the slavery epithet into each other's faces.

Brothers of the human race, East, West, North, and South, let us lay aside passion, enmity, and spite, and bring to our rescue all the wisdom, science, and art that we possess. For only by means of these, and the aid of our common Father and God—Material Nature—can evil be displaced by good.

When the Roman Catholic phase of supernaturalism was breaking up, those in authority perpetrated deeds which all remember with horror, and which constructive revolutionists and comprehensive thinkers look back on with humili-

ation, regret, and pity, near akin to shame that they belong
to the human race. Now that supernaturalism itself is
breaking up, let those in power, especially in the "Model
Republic," take warning by the past, and not commit deeds
that will consign them to the agonies of remorse, unless they
are, considering the age in which they live, unpardonably
ignorant, and send their names to posterity coupled with
such execrations as are heaped on those of the infernally
Holy Inquisitors and their governmental abettors, most of
whom unquestionably were, however, far more sincere and
conscientious than any human tormentors can now claim to
be.

### § 13. PENAL CODES THEIR OWN NEMESIS.

Throughout the whole domain of science, nothing *can* be
more certain, than that the amount of criminality *justly*
chargeable to an individual, cannot exceed the proportion
which such individual's power bears to the power of the
whole human race. Therefore penal statutes are as consummate quackery as a continual application of the scalpel's
edge to the external manifestations of small pox, in order
to effect a cure, would be.

What! charge the iniquity of all mankind to a single
individual, and, with a force of a thousand millions against
one, murder an unresisting prisoner in cool blood? *Deliberately*, and with assassinous intent, twist a rough hemp-cord
around the tender neck of a defenceless human victim, till
the joints are dislocated, the eye-balls forced from their
sockets, the tongue squeezed horribly from the mouth,
the facial veins burst, and death, as if in pity, ends the
agony?

And, sometimes (unless 'tis an infernal dream), "man," (?)
armed, and *regularly commissioned* by the power and
authority of the whole State, draws the murderous halter
around the fair neck of — — — WOMAN! Is "Earth,"
*really*, Hell? Are "human beings," *in truth*, Devil-incar-
nations?

In *deliberately* "punishing crime," society commits an
act that degrades man far below beasts; none of whom
inflict death, or any lesser evil, without the plea of necessity,
instinct, passion, or accident. But it will not be long before
science will *transcend* that erring mountebank, reason, in
the government of mankind.

But I am not going to *minutely* examine and expose the
fallacy of " punishing " " crime." That would require a large

volume. I mean to thrust straight home to the very heart of this abomination; to show in a very few words, that the blindly malicious and stupid advocates of "punishment" defeat their own *professed* aims; that all penalties, *in addition* to those which *necessarily* follow a breach of *real* law, augment the very evils they are applied to cure, and in an exact ratio, other things being equal, to their severity.

The death-penalty *always* elevates the sufferer thereof to a hero; *generally* to a saint; and *often* to a martyr. As to its preventive effects: Treason involves this penalty; yet our "Model Republic" was spawned of treason, and several of the States which compose it are now in the midst of the very saturnalia of treason, if we are to take for their representatives those whom popular rule has *de facto* constituted such.*

"Hang the demagogues who are now preaching treason, and every mobocrat they head," say the short-sighted friends of our miserable apology for "law and order," in the very face and eyes of the wholesale failure of their favorite scheme.

Nay, sirs, let's have no more hanging. If you *must* have *some* revenge on those who have *immediately* disturbed that chronic armistice that the world calls *peace!* for the last few weeks, † who have thus damaged the public prosperity to the amount, to speak within bounds, of more than it would cost to build the Pacific railroad, and created a riot that will not probably end without murder, let me propose a substitute for the hanging or even imprisoning scheme, and let this be the last vestige of punishment that man can inflict on his fellow man. Only in *that* hope would I propose it. The horrible side of the punishment enormity has long and ably been held up. I will try what exposing its absurdity can effect.

Let the order-abiding portion of the community, if they *must* have *some* revengeful "satisfaction" for past offences, "enact" a "law" (and let this be the last "law" ever

---

* A government, the *real* agent of the people, never existed. When those whom the caucus and ballot-box scheme declares the people's agents happen to be honest, when they refuse to accept the bribe of a clique or an individual to pass this or that law, or pursue this or that measure, it is a mere matter of generosity—a sort of imperially exercised grace. Let any one watch the lobby during a session of the Legislature; or, if he could, get access to the private conferences which our Presidents, Governors, Mayors, and "elected" Judges hold, and see who the *real* governors of all Democracies and Republics are.

† This was written January 8, 1861.

"enacted") that all demagogues whose machinations have
disturbed the *usual* tranquillity, or who shall have willfully
originated, or in any way assisted, schemes whereby the
public have been either swindled or hoaxed, under pretext
of government, and such of the mob who have maliciously
followed them as can be caught, together with all who have
*voluntarily* aided or abetted them, either openly or *surreptitiously*, directly or *indirectly*, shall be publicly turned butt
end upward over some official knee, and, after a prayer by
some devout clergyman, have their bare posteriors solemnly
spanked by the *hands* of the common hangman.

This would not be a martyrdom that *any* one would be
proud of having suffered, and it would be a perfect damper.
to all heroism in the case.   Not even the sword and epaulets
of a cavalier whose seat of honor had, in accordance with
"law and order," been publicly hand-slapped, would cause
a lady's hand to wave, or her heart to sigh.

And would any demagogue who had, with all the for-
malities of "law" and "religion," had his bare butt-end
publicly spanked, ever "stump it" afterward?   Could the
gravity of *any* audience stand the sight of the *face* of an
orator who had compulsorily, yet *legally*, appeared before
them with his *breech* uppermost, and with that most comical
substitute for his gammon-laboratory *respectfully uncovered?*
Would not the reminiscences that would spontaneously
arise, cause irrepressible laughter to drown the most bunkum
eloquence?

The law here recommended is less brutal and shameful
than the one we now have, by the vast difference between
breaking men's necks and a moderate application of the open
hand to a rather insensible part.   And I earnestly ask all who
are capable of judging in the case, if they do not candidly
believe that if these spanked *political* burglars, swindlers,
thieves, or humbugs, resorted to the pen, instead of to the
rostrum or stump, they, and all aspirants for public office,
would take better care than they ever have done that their
schemes in behalf of the sovereignty of the dear people,
and for enlarging the area of freedom, should not be
treacheries gotten up to serve their own mean, narrow, mis-
taken interests, well knowing that if they brought disaster
on the country, they would, as some slight compensation,
have to furnish it with laughing-stocks and *butts* for
ridicule?

I most earnestly invite our honorable judges, particularly
our chief justices, our worthy President of the United

States, and equally worthy Mayor of New York, together
with some of our most *prominent* members of Congress and
of the Common Council of our city aforesaid, to consider
the feasibility, and contemplate the effect, of trying the
experiment of such a "law" as I have proposed, on several
hundred of the most infernal "scoundrels" in this country.

Don't let me be thought joking. I solemnly protest that
I never was more serious in my life than I am, in declaring
that it is my unshakable conviction, that if even *common*
murderers, brigands, and thieves were treated with that
mild barbarity I have just pleaded for in behalf of wholesale
"criminals," murderers would be less common than now,
meaner criminals would decrease, and those who still per-
sisted would be far less dangerous to society than they are
after being goaded to desperation by a few years' torture in
our infernal prisons.

Away with punishment altogether. It's a disgrace to
countries as barbarous as Algiers or Dahomey. The most
benighted tribe in Africa has nothing more savage. 'Tis
a legacy we inherited from savagism itself, and society
becomes ashamed of it, and drops its practice exactly in
proportion as man becomes refined. The last relic of it will
cease, when man is perfected.

Let the *great*, but *most simple* truth, that no breach of
*real* law ever *did* or ever *can* avoid its *due* penalty, that
the interests of the human race are inseparably connected,
and that nature will, through science, art, and lower material
development, prove all-sufficient, be erected into a creed,
taught in Sunday-schools, and made universally public, and
let *consistent action* be taken thereon, and all transgression,
from the meanest to that of even national magnificence,
will soon cease.

Needs there any argument or demonstration to prove
that inflicting evil on evil only augments evil? Surely
nothing can be more absurd and ridiculous than revenge.

The true cause of "crime," or "moral evil," is, that
creation is incomplete. The parts of the Universal Organism, or all which *to, in* and *through* man exists, have got to
be adjusted so that they will not *clash;* so that they will
not *chafe,* even; and man has got to do this. He has got
to finish creation—to set it in order, before he can be
accommodated therein. For he is the *sensible* head of all
in his connection. His is the highest *intelligible* intelligence. The instant we talk about mind abstracted from its
material organs, our words have clean parted company

with meaning, and we find ourselves sinking deeper and deeper into the bottomless depths of nonsense.*

If the wheels, and springs and cranks of a cutlery manufactory should clash, and chafe, and injure each other, what epithet, but that of fool, or madman, would be applied to those who had charge of it, should they fly into a passion, expel some, and bend and break others, in order to make them work right? Or, if the faultiness was very bad, treat the whole building to volleys of musketry and broadsides of cannon, in order to mend matters? Would not such overseers be considered only fit to tenant a madhouse? Well, *fur worse* fools and madmen are the penal law-givers who have charge of that embodiment of all the complications of mechanism—the Social Organism. The conditions for good must be provided, before good *can* result, equally in the case of man, or in that of coarser materiality. And all attempts to promote well-doing, except according to this rule, are folly or quackery, and *must* result, as they always have done, in *failure*, or worse calamity.

"Evil," or "crime," will wholly cease, only when the whole human race form one Social Organism, governed by those scientific enough to know that any malpractice on their part, will be suicidal, and so perfectly fitted to the Universal Organism, or all in man's connection, as to control it to the extent that to desire will be to have, with the exception (if it can truly be called an exception) of just exertion enough to give due value to possession, and that individual conscious existence will continue till all the varieties of happiness presentable to the five senses, exhaust their value by repetition.

Leaders of mankind, your true function is to organize all this; and when you set yourselves about it dispassionately, scientifically, and in a workmanly manner, you will realize Heaven on Earth so suddenly, that the only wonder will be that it had not been done before.

---

* The beautiful and regular pictures of shrubbery which the crystallization of frost forms on the sidewalk after a sudden thaw, is sufficient, in the case of such as have understandings more comprehensive than are those of the masses, to nullify all the arguments that can be adduced to prove "the existence of the *supernatural* designer," about whom the apostles of mystery and balderdash have so long astounded their hearers, whilst picking their pockets.

THE END.

# LIBERAL BOOKS

# CALVIN BLANCHARD,

## 76 NASSAU STREET, N. Y.

*Sent by mail, postage free, on receipt of retail price. Thirty per cent. discount to Booksellers, or to those who buy at one time as many as would amount, at retail prices, to $20. Never sold at Trade Sales or other Auctions.*

NOTICE.—Utterly opposed to the abominable method of doing business which degrades credit to the most mischievous gambling, holds out every possible inducement to fraud, and treacherously victimizes the inveterately honest : CALVIN BLANCHARD will, until those delusive, honor-deadening SHAMS of law for collecting debts are abolished, adhere strictly to the CASH ON DELIVERY system of trade.

[**C. B. keeps constantly for sale, more than 30,000 volumes in every department of Literature, Science, and Art, at astonishingly low Prices.**]

--------

## Strauss' Critical Examination of the Life of Jesus.

Translated from the fourth German edition by MARIAN EVANS. In two royal octavo volumes, pp. 902. With a fine steel Portrait. $4 50.

"The most formidable assailant of the ecclesiastical theology of Christ-endom."—*Theodore Parker.*

It most learnedly and completely unveils the mythical substructure of that compound of Bhoodism, Judaism, and Paganism, called Christianity.

## The Positive Philosophy of Auguste Comte.

Translated by HARRIET MARTINEAU. In one elegant royal octavo volume, pp. 838. With a fine steel Portrait. $3.

## Comte's Social Physics. With Portrait, 25c.

"Comte is the Bacon of the nineteenth century. Like Bacon, he fully sees the cause of our intellectual anarchy, and also sees the cure. No one before him ever dreamed of treating social problems otherwise than upon theological or metaphysical methods. He first showed how possible—nay, how imperative—it was that social questions should be treated on the same footing with all other scientific questions. We have no hesitation in recording our conviction that the ' *Cours de Philosophie Positive* ' (Positive Philosophy) is the greatest work of our century."—*Lewes's Biographical History of Philosophy.*

" A work which only requires to be better known to place its author in the very highest class of European thinkers. * * * A sociological system widely removed from the vague and conjectural character of

1

all former attempts, and worthy to take its place, at last, among established sciences. * * * A work which I hold to be far the greatest
yet produced in the Philosophy of the Sciences."—*Mill's System of Logic.*

"A work of profound science, marked with great acuteness of reason-
ing, and conspicuous for the highest attributes of intellectual power.
Under the head of *Social Physics*, the author treats of the general structure of human societies, of the fundamental natural law of the development of the human species, and of the progress of civilization. This
last section is subdivided into three heads—the THEOLOGICAL EPOCH, the
METAPHYSICAL EPOCH, and the POSITIVE EPOCH—the first of these embracing FETISHISM, POLYTHEISM, and MONOTHEISM."—*Sir David Brewster.*

### The Essence of Christianity. By LUDWIG FEUERBACH.
Translated from the second German edition, by MARIAN EVANS.
Large 12mo. $1 50.

This is the most powerful materialistic work ever written. It is the
natural history of supernaturalism—the key to the cypher of the theological enigma; a complete demolisher of all metaphysical or transcendental
theories. Feuerbach's masterly explanation of the religious idea, makes
his work, like the writings of Comte and Fourier, indispensable to *practical* social artists, to all who would know how to *eliminate* superstition.

The yearning of man after something which he supposes to be only
*supernaturally* attainable, is an earnest of *natural* success; of the perfection to which through natural science, art, and development, he will
arrive. This is in accordance with Fourier's great axiom, that "attrac-
tions are proportioned to destinies." Man has his God in himself; he is
a progressive being; the true meaning of miracle is development;
through which, man will be substantially the Almighty which he creates
his abstract subjectivity. For man *cannot* look beyond nature, and yet
he *does look to perfection.*

### The Social Destiny of Man; or, Theory of the Four
Movements. By CHARLES FOURIER. 8vo., pp. 422, with Portrait.
$1 50 in cloth, $1 in paper covers.

Demonstrates the feasibility of an arrangement between labor, capital
and skill, which shall make capital *perfectly* secure, and immeasurably
more valuable than now; which shall make skill operate for, instead of
against labor, and at the same time fully secure its own interests; which
shall give constant employment and ample remuneration to labor; which
shall banish pauperism and "crime," regulate the sexual relations so as
to *satisfy* instead of *repressing the natural* passions, and put an end to
prostitution, wife and husband poisoning, seduction, and even *mental
adultery*

---

## ART-LIBERTY BOOKS.
#### "ALL NATURE IS BUT ART LESS UNDERSTOOD."—*Pope.*

### The Religion of Science; or, The Art of Actualizing Li-
berty, and of Perfecting, and Sufficiently Prolonging Happiness:
Being a Practical Answer to the Great Question—"If you take
away my Religion, what will you give me in its stead?" 12mo. 87c.

### The Essence of Science; or, The Catechism of Positive So-
ciology and Physical Mentality. 12mo. 60c. and 37c.

### The New Crisis; or, Our Deliverance from Priestly Fraud.
Political Charlatanry and Popular Despotism. 13c.

**Hell on Earth!** Murder, Rape, Robbery, Swindling and Forgery Covertly Organized. Cannibalism made Dainty ! An Exposure of the Infernal Machinations and Horrible Atrocities of Whited Sepulcherism ; together with A Sure Plan for its Speedy Overthrow. 18c.

**The Life of Thomas Paine,** Mover of the "Declaration of Independence ;" Secretary of Foreign Affairs under the first American Congress; Member of the National Convention of France ; Author of "Common Sense," "The Crisis," "Rights of Man," "Age of Reason," etc.: THE MAN, whose motto was " *The World is my Country; to do good, my Religion.*" Embracing *Practical Considerations on Human Rights ;* demonstrating that *Man tends irrepressibly to Actual Freedom ;* and showing *A Liberty-Aim Connection* in the action of the World's Three Great Author-Heroes—ROUSSEAU, PAINE, and COMTE. By the Author of "The Religion of Science." With elegantly engraved Portraits of Rousseau, Paine, and Comte. 12mo , cloth. 50c.

The five preceding works are all by the same author. He takes the ground that "Free Government can be nothing less than the Art of Arts, to which True Religion must be its corresponding Science of Sciences; and they who preach liberty from any other stand-point, are either circumscribed, weak, deluded, or so abominably corrupt, and so blind to *true* self-interest, as to mean spoils;" that "nature is all-sufficient;" that therefore, "through science, art, and spontaneous development, the highest theories will prove to be practicabilities." For "subjectivity cannot transcend objectivity; ideas are not innate, or supersensuous; mind, will, desire, are functional of material organism, and cannot, therefore, wander beyond nature. Man is the highest organism; he is nature's head; his will, therefore, *really is nature's will ;* and nature's will *must* be the measure of her power and of her resources, and these *must* be adequate to the realization of the highest conceivable bliss ; and the religious instinct which mentally distinguishes man from lower animals, is the index which points to the goal of development—to *complete creation.* The human race, therefore, will achieve on earth the perfection of happiness which man now mistakenly looks for after death. Men and women will be as beautiful and every way as perfect as "angels " are imagined to be; and life will, by natural means, be so lengthened that perfect happiness will last till all the varieties of it which can be presented to the five senses exhaust their value by repetition. *"Heaven,"* and *"eternal* happiness" are but glimmering, distance-dimmed views of the *veritable* "Paradise " which science, art, and spontaneous development will secure to man in this substantial sphere."

No other writer has so clearly shown *how to eliminate theology,* and its loathsome train of moral, political and social evils.

---

**The Creed of Christendom:** Its Foundations and Superstructure. By WILLIAM RATHBONE GREG. $1 25.

" No candid reader of the ' Creed of Christendom ' can close the book without the secret acknowledgment that it is a model of honest investigation and clear exposition; that it is conceived in the true spirit of serious and faithful research; and that whatever the author wants of being an ecclesiastical Christian, is plainly not essential to the noble guidance of life, and the devout earnestness of the affections."—*Westminster Review.*

**The Doctrine of Inspiration:** Being an Inquiry concerning the Infallibility, Inspiration and Authority of Holy Writ. By the Rev. JOHN MACNAUGHT, M.A. Oxon., Incumbent of St. Chrysostom's Church, Everton, Liverpool. 12mo. $1 37.

"This work is more significant than any which has appeared since the advent of Strauss' 'Life of Jesus.' The vulgar idea of the supernatural inspiration of the Bible is here abandoned; and what is more, it is shown that many of the chief dignitaries, including four bishops of the Church of England, have held, *on the sly*, similar opinions. The citadel of Christian superstition may *now* be considered as *authoritatively* surrendered.

"It is the first book written by an orthodox clergyman which decidedly denies the doctrine of Scriptural infallibility. It is well written and manly."—*Christian Inquirer* [*Unitarian*].

**What is Truth?** or, Revelation its own Nemesis. 12mo. $1.

"The writer of these letters, in reply to the everlasting enigma, leaves not one stone upon another of the Christian temple; he rests not until he has created for himself a new heaven and a new earth, until he can kneel down a solitary worshipper at the shrine of justice.

"We would especially recommend these letters to the more calm, but not less convinced author of 'Miracles and Science,' as they contain the strongest and most searching objections to which the orthodox scheme is exposed."—*Leader.*

**New Researches on Ancient History:** Embracing an Examination of the History of the Jews until the Captivity of Babylon; and showing the origin of the Mosaic Legends concerning the Creation, Fall of Man, Flood and Confusion of Languages. By C. F. VOLNEY, Count and Peer of France; Author of "The Ruins, or Meditations on the Revolutions of Empires," etc., etc. Handsome 12mo., muslin. $1 25.

**Volney's Ruins;** or, Meditations on the Revolutions of Empires. To which is added "The Law of Nature," "The Controversy between Dr. Priestley and Volney," and a Biographical Notice. 50c. in cloth, 30c. in paper covers.

**Mary Wollstonecraft's Vindication of the Rights** OF WOMAN, with Strictures on Political and Moral Subjects. With a Biographical Sketch of the Author. One beautiful volume, 12mo. 75c.

**Vestiges of Civilization;** or, The Ætiology of History, Religious, Æsthetical, Political, and Philosophical. 12mo. $1 25.

**History of Priestcraft in all Ages and Nations.** By WILLIAM HOWITT. 12mo. 75c.

**A New System of Phrenology.** By JOHN S. HITTELL. 12mo. 75c.

**A Plea for Pantheism.** By JOHN S. HITTELL 25c.

**The Evidences against Christianity.** By JOHN S. HIT-
TELL. In two large 12mo. volumes. $2 50.

**The Odic-Magnetic Letters of Baron Reichenbach.**
Translated from the German by JOHN S. HITTELL. 37c.

**Somnambulism and Cramp.** By BARON REICHENBACH.
Translated by JOHN S. HITTELL. 12mo. $1.

**The Devil's Pulpit;** or, A Series of Astro-Theological Sermons (some of which were heretofore published in "The Beacon"),
by the Rev. ROBERT TAYLOR, B.A., author of the "Diegesis," "Syn-
tagma," etc. With a Sketch of his Life, and an Astronomical Introduction. One handsome volume, 12mo. Price $1 25.

**Taylor's Astro-Theological Lectures,** being the second
series of the Devil's Pulpit, 12mo. $1 37.

**Taylor's Belief** *not* **the Safe Side,** 10c.

**Taylor's Lectures on Free Masonry,** 25c.
Robert Taylor was one of those rare geniuses in whose writings the
most laughter-provoking wit was blended with great learning and profound research. He shows that all the modern interpretations of the
"Holy Scriptures" are no more their original meaning, than the lines,
curves, points, circles, angles, etc., etc., of mathematicians are mathemati-
cal science. He has found the key to these Scriptures, and clearly shows
what the sacred writers *did* mean. In his writings he incidentally embodies the substance of Du Puy's great work—"*Origin of all Religions.*"

**The Mystical Quaternity Analyzed;** or, Who is the
Lord God? By ROBERT TAYLOR. 30 cents.

Who was Jesus Christ? By an able critic. 10 cents.

Who is the Holy Ghost? By ROBERT TAYLOR. 10 cents.

Who is the Devil? By ROBERT TAYLOR. 15 cents.

**Thomas Paine's Theological and Political Works,**
together with HIS LIFE, by the author of "The Religion of Science."
2 vols.,12mo., $2 00.

**Thomas Paine's Political Works.** 1 vol., 12mo., $1 00.

**Thomas Paine's Theological Works.** Together with
HIS LIFE, by the author of "The Religion of Science." 1 vol.,
12mo., $1 00.

**Thomas Paine's Age of Reason,** in paper cover, 25c.; in
cloth, 37 cents.
All the above volumes of Paine's Works, together with his Life,
have just been published on large, new type, on very fine paper, and
in substantial binding. Each volume has a fine steel portrait of
Paine, and the Life (for the full title, see another part of this Catalogue) has fine portraits of Rousseau, Paine, and Comte.

**How to get a Divorce;** together with the Laws of all
the States of the Union on this subject, and an able plea in favor
of Free-Love, or Passional Emancipation. By a Member of the
New York Bar. 25 cents.

**The Divine and Moral Works of Plato,** translated from the original Greek, with Introductory Dissertations and Notes. First American, from the Sixth London edition, carefully revised and corrected from Sydenham and Taylor. $1 25.

This work embodies the spiritual doctrines and moral sentiments of Christianism, and the disciples of Jesus have always been sorely puzzled to find out how all this came to be known five hundred years before the birth of their Saviour, whose Gospel "brought life and immortality," and such "sublime *moral* precepts" "to light." The earlier popes made strenuous efforts to suppress the works of Plato and Aristotle.

**A Message to The "Sovereign People" of The United States;** exhibiting to Their Majesties the Infernal Treachery or worse Inability of their Religious Counsellors and of their Political "Servants," proving the Identity of the Theological and Ethical Delusions, exposing the Elective Franchise Hoax, and Revealing a New and Self-Evidently Efficient Remedy for Superstition, Despotism and Evil. A Pamphlet of 46 octavo pages. By Calvin Blanchard. 10 cents. 15 copies for $1 00.

☞ *All the profits on this publication will be expended in furnishing Clergymen and Politicians with copies thereof gratis.*

**Thorndale;** or, The Conflict of Opinions. By Wm. Smith, author of "A Discourse on Ethics." $1 25.

**Vestiges of the Natural History of Creation.** Handsome 12mo. 75 cents.

**Hobbes (Thomas),** The Complete Works of. Elegant London Edition, in 16 volumes, octavo. $16 00.

☞ Published at $50. Not sent by mail. Only a few copies. No discount on this work.

**A Review of "The Trials of a Mind, in its Progress to Catholicism."** By an ex-Clergyman. 12mo. 75c.

**History of the Institution of the Sabbath Day;** Its Uses and Abuses. With Notices of the Puritans, Quakers, etc. By William Logan Fisher. 12mo. 62c.

**Introduction to Social Science.** By George H. Calvert. 12mo. 50c.

**Mysticism and its Results.** Being an Inquiry into the Uses and Abuses of Secrecy. By John Delafield, Esq. 12mo. 37c.

**Conciliation Naturelle du Droit et du Devoir.** Par Henri Disdier, Avocat. 2 vols., royal 8vo., pp. 1255. $2.

---

## PASSIONAL BOOKS.

*(Indispensable to students of progress, and the safest that can be put into the hands of those who read for amusement, as I shall demonstrate.)*

**The Confessions of Jean Jacques Rousseau.** A New Translation, in which not a word of the original is omitted, nor its meaning in any way altered. Two beautiful 12mo. volumes, cloth gilt, price $2 50.

The London edition of "Rousseau's Confessions" was so scandalously deficient of the most *recherché* passages that the present publisher rejected it altogether, and had the whole work translated afresh, by an able scholar, from the French edition of Madame George Sand, wherein had been faithfully restored, from the original manuscript sold to the French Government by Rousseau's widow, all the passages which, when such "*virtuous*" rulers as Robespierre and Marat governed France, were omitted. Reader, the most charming and instructive feat which composition ever performed is here truly and faithfully reëxhibited. Jean Jacques alone has dared to bare the innermost secrets of the human heart, and to expose to just abhorrence the abominations which theological moralism had perverted human nature into enacting.

"There hardly exists such another example of the miracles which composition can perform."—*Lord Brougham.*

"There have been what purported to be translations of the world-famous Confessions of Rousseau before; but Mr. Calvin Blanchard's is the first that we know of which is unmutilated and accurate."—*Putnam's Monthly.*

"It has been translated into every language in Europe; the librarian of Napoleon devoted a large volume to the classification of the different editions of it."—*Ev. Post.*

**Boccaccio's Decameron;** or, Ten Days' Entertainment. In one beautiful 18mo. vol., pp. 500, with 18 fine steel engravings. $1.

The gayest and most gallant literary feast that ever regaled human taste. Rehearsing The Decameron kept a large party of fair ladies and gallant gentlemen in such a thrill of delight, that the plague which ravaged Florence in 1348, passed harmlessly by them. That prince of old fogies, grim Death himself, chuckled for once and hurried on.

**The Library of Love.** In three neat pocket volumes, pp. 803, with fine steel engravings. Sold separately at 50c. each, or $1 50 the set. The most amorous and recherché effusions ever penned. Comprising :

I. OVID'S ART OF LOVE, and Amorous Works entire.

II. BASIA ; The Kisses of Joannes Secundus and Jean Bonnefons.

III. FABLES FROM BOCCACCIO AND CHAUCER. By JOHN DRYDEN.

In THE CONFESSIONS, THE DECAMERON, and THE LIBRARY OF LOVE, are fairly, openly and perfectly exhibited, the *hitherto and now* workings, under the difficulties which old fogyism throws in its way, of the tender passion to which sentient beings are indebted for their existence.

Yet to such a pitch has false religion perverted the rationality of the highest order of sentient beings, that *some* of them are too "*chaste*" to read any of the said works except *privately;* and so *very* "modest" as to try to prevent everybody but themselves from reading them at all!

And stranger still, *some* even, who flatter themselves that they have abandoned false religion, do yet so cling to that insidious phase of it—moralism—that they continue to imagine *ignorance* to be a safer guardian for virtue than *knowledge!* Oh, how ineradicable is inbred falsehood.

I would insure young ladies and gentlemen against the traps and pitfalls to which present institutions expose them, who have read every book in my Catalogue, for half the premium for which I would underwrite those whose natural feelings have been so repressed, that pent-up lust crimsons their cheeks with blushes, and casts down their eye-glances with shame, on reading the holy text—"Before the *rooster* crows twice, thou shalt deny me thrice."

The New York Tribune, in the course of its remarks on the elopement of Mary Gurney, the wife of a rich London banker, with her groom, most wisely says :

" The fashionable mode of treatment may be summed up in the terse injunctions, ' Cover up !' ' Keep dark !' Let all reputable people shut their eyes to the innumerable escapades, ignore (so far as possible) their existence, and keep all knowledge of them, to the extent of our ability, from the minds of our children, but especially of our daughters. And it was under the influence of this system that Mary Gurney, herself an illegitimate child and the offspring of an elopement, was reared. * * * We believe the system to be radically wrong and practically disastrous. We believe it no more desirable to seal the eyes of the young to the fact of the existence of Adultery than to that of the existence of Murder."

The passional books which I publish, including even Fourier on the Sexual Relations, excite no morbid or unnatural curiosity ; for if, in Rousseau's Confessions, priests and celibats are exposed for unnatural conduct, it is always in such a way as to excite disgust therefor. Rousseau confesses that his discoveries in that direction well nigh cured him of a most unnatural habit. They do not present such conduct as *natural* or *common*, as certain law-books, contrived by the most treacherous malice, or by consummate ignorance, and accessible to all curious youth, do ; nor, above all, as heaven-sanctioned, as the Bible leaves it plainly to be inferred that the conduct of "righteous" Lot's family was.

Reformers should consider themselves as physicians to the social organism. And how are physicians to find out how to apply effectual remedies without studying the symptoms which their patients exhibit.

These Passional Books, studied in connection with Plato, the ablest expounder of the ethical code which has not altered a particle to this day, show what a miserable quack nostrum moralism is. It was a perfect abortion from the beginning, as all will discover who read Ovid. They show the disastrous effects of attempting to repress the natural, and by far the strongest and most imperious of human passions. Should this knowledge be smothered? Surely thoughtlessness, insanity or idiocy are the only pleas which can save those who contend that it should be, from being justly accused as the malicious emissaries of evil, treacherously disguised as the ministers of good.

These books show that society must pursue a radically different course with the human passions. They show that the human desires cannot be conquered; that attempting even to repress them, only causes them to raise the very devil. And what a horribly dull, monotonous, stupid and dreary world this would be, if the raid of moralists against gallantry should prove a complete success. If a scheme of monogamy could be invented, whereby all sexual intercourse out of it would be impossible, does *any one* suppose that such a scheme would not upset monogamy itself, in twenty-four hours' time, no matter what the consequences might be? Adultery, fornication, and prostitution, are absolutely inseparable from monogamy; they are as much its counterpart as the Devil is the complement of Christianism. Moralists *naively* confess this; they confess that the above " vices " are " necessary evils "—evils which *they* despair of curing. " Necessary evils?" 'Tis the most abominable lie ever uttered. 'Tis the most horrible blasphemy that by any possible form of words can be perpetrated.

Is it not, then, matter of legitimate mirth, that the love passions circumvent, by *any* means, all the machinations of gloomy, unnatural, depraved, abhorrent, blasphemous old fogyism ? that they show their ability to *compel* the doctors of the social organism to study till they find out how to unobstruct the course of natural law, and render its operation harmonious and good?

Down, I say down, with those *guardians of social corruption*, hypocrisy, makebelieve and cant. Away with that immaculate abortion—that most insidious treachery; that complete clog in the way of *practical good*—moralism. Man wants the SCIENCE AND ART OF WELL-DOING, Nothing short of this will avail.

# MY UNDERTAKING AND ITS AUSPICES.

In 1854, Comte's Positive Philosophy and Feuerbach's Essence of Christianity fell under my observation. Many years before, I had read Fourier. His system, by itself, however, seemed to me to lack foundation. But Comte furnished that foundation, and Feuerbach's demonstration of the naturalness of "supernaturalism" precluded the possibility of *my* coming to any other conclusion in the premises than that the religious idea was the index to, and nature's guaranty for, that Heaven on earth, of which Fourier was the prophet; but which he, unfortunately, attempted to minutely describe at too great a distance, and thus fell into vagaries, with respect to particulars, which did much to obscure, and bring into contempt, his most profound and transcendently brilliant discoveries.

I now determined to do all that lay in my power to forward that human perfection which was no longer a mere vague abstraction, but a mathematically calculable certainty. I soon placed before the American public, "*The Positive Philosophy*" of Auguste Comte, "The Essence of Christianity," by Ludwig Feuerbach, and *Fourier's* "*Social Destiny of Man.*"

It is but justice to Messrs. D. Appleton & Co. to say that before I commenced publishing liberal books, they imported an edition of The Positive Philosophy; a work as much more powerful in the destruction of theology, than anything before written, as Sharp's rifles and artillery are more destructive than pop-guns and bows and arrows.

Also, the Messrs. Harper & Brothers had the honor to precede me in the publication of "Howitt's History of Priestcraft." They also, as I do, publish that silencer of Moses—that most powerful antidote to superstition, priestcraft, and old fogyism, "*Vestiges of the Natural History of Creation.*"

In fact, the largest publishers both in France, Germany, England, and the United States are finding it for their interest to publish, not only the most thorough of what are vulgarly called "infidel books," but even those books which recognize the *rights of the human passions*. To such an extent have passional rights come to be respected, that our most fashionable periodicals increased their circulation immensely by laying before their readers that unanswerable plea for the freedom of the affections, purporting to be a letter from the *truly* Honorable Mrs. Mary Gurney.

Do the Harpers, the Browns, the Littles, the Bohns, the Appletons, the Longmans, and the numerous other eminent publishers who are putting forth books which are sapping the very foundation of " our holy religion " in a "*quiet way,*" as their Christian (?) apologists term it, *sincerely* believe what they profess to ? When *I* professed the religion of Christianity (which was only whilst I remained ignorant of the fact that its truth had been *understandingly* disputed), I was as sincere as I am now that I profess the religion of science; and I most solemnly declare, that I would have suffered martyrdom in its most horrible form, sooner than I would have published Higgins's "Anacalypsis," Comte's "Positive Philosophy," Theodore Parker's works, Buckle's "History of Civilization in England," "Hume's Essays," the "Vestiges of Creation," Howitt's "History of Priestcraft," Humboldt's "Letters to Von Ense," or hundreds of similar works now put forth in "*a quiet way,*" by Christian (?) publishers. I most earnestly entreat the Christian (?) apologists, for the "*quiet*" method of "damning souls" and

" demoralizing mankind," to reflect one moment on the character of the scheme which they are apologizing for. Do but this, and whatever may be your conclusions as to religion, you will respect, aye, love me ever afterward for this hint.

The " Essence of Science " I published in 1859, and " The Religion of Science " in 1860. These give a view of the results which a practical application of Comte, Feuerbach and Fourier must produce. They show conclusively, that *nature* is sufficient; that she spontaneously tends to perfection. And they demonstrate how man can so facilitate the process, that this great aim of nature may be attained with rapid and constantly increasing speed. Up to the present time, so great has been the demand for books, liberal not only with respect to opposition to theology and its governmental superstructure, but with respect to the long-crushed rights of the human passions, that my publications are now forty-four in number, of large size on the average, and many of them have, without recourse to auction sales or to the fraudulent and gambling credit system, reached their fifth edition.

## THE CLERGY ARE COMING ROUND.

The clergy have been most encouraging purchasers of my books, as their preaching attests. Scarcely a discourse do they deliver in which they do not allude to some of them, *or their contents*, and in a manner exactly calculated to arouse curiosity respecting, and to stir up inquiry for them. The best points in their sermons are suggested by my publications, as all know who have heard the one and read the other. The books which I publish, and similar ones, are now far more consulted by the higher clergy than is the Bible itself. Evidently, they long to be able to preach the religion of science, to expand the infant mind by means of it, instead of cramping it all but to death within the narrow compass of the religion of mystery. As, throughout nature, the good which is capable of arising from use, is in exact proportion to the evil which arises from abuse, what conceivable good may we not with certainty expect from that now most abominable of abuses, the church?

## THE RICH ARE WAKING UP.

From the wealthy—from those who are heartily sick of the mockery of the gilding which little more than hides their misery from those who cannot afford whitewash for theirs—who see that the way which I am showing is the only one whereby wealth can be made valuable to any extent worth mentioning, have I also received most substantial support. But I must not mention names. We must "wait *a little* longer " (and I am encouraged to think not *very* long) before it will be *popularly* glorious to reward the toils and strengthen the hands of those who are laboring for the religion of science and its *practical liberty and goodness.*

## THE LADIES ARE ON MY SIDE.

Terrified by superstition, and brow-beaten and constrained by old fogyism, their silver-toned voices and sweet lips may falter out No, but their ravishing eyes say Yes. Their inmost heart-aspirations are for the triumph of a religious and social system which will develop them beyond a blemish; thus banishing their jealousies of each other, and rendering them very goddesses at whose feet it will be the highest bliss of man, commensurately developed, to adore. In their inmost hearts, they long for the time when love will be universally reciprocal, and when lovers may, secure from harm and consequent disgrace, spontaneously luxuriate in each other's embraces.

## ALL THE WORLD IS WITH ME.

Mankind express their fears that the *intelligible* perfection which I, an apostle of the religion of science, preach, is "*too good to be true.*" They thus *naïvely* own that their very hearts' desire is for the triumph of the religion of science and for *my success.* Is not happiness the wish of all? Can any one object to Heaven on earth? Why believe in a Millennium incomprehensibly producible, instead of in one demonstrably practicable?

## THE OLD FOGIES

even do not hate me; they but delude themselves when they think so. Man's own ignorance is the only thing which he *really* hates. It is his ignorance alone which stands between him and perfect. and sufficiently lasting happiness; ignorance with respect to the modifications and harmonies of which the *substantial* is precisely as susceptible as that figment of the imagination, the "*spiritual,*" is incoherently fancied to be. There is, there *can be,* no despotism, no evil, of which the kind of ignorance just named is not the sole cause.

## THE PRESS IS MY ALLY.

### *The Religious Press, even, indirectly aids me!*

## THE DAILY "WORLD,"

a newspaper unctuous of holiness, in an elaborate general notice of all the books published by me, says that they are "without suppression," and that I have "wit enough to see that honesty is the best policy;" which high eulogium contrasts ludicrously enough with its author's simultaneous *feint* of reproving me for my course as a publisher.

Is it a rare specimen of "honesty," and therefore deserving of special praise, for an *American* publisher to put forth books of vital importance to mankind "without suppression?" Have either of the editors of "The World" (one of whom I am told is a "*Shakspeare Scholar*") ever been employed in mutilating European books for the edification of the American public, a public which glories in nothing so much as in being its own best judge in all matters pertaining to religion, government and morals?

The censorship of the press is so odious, that it has to be exercised with great caution and due formality, even in *imperial France.* Do publishers, in "*free*" America, dare to erect themselves into the most insufferable of tyrants? And am I the only publisher on whom this great Democratic Republic can safely rely? "*The World's*" praise is either alarmingly significant, or altogether too complimentary. I am well assured that the views of "The World," *sub rosâ,* both with respect to "the flesh" and "the devil," are "*all right,*" that its whole body editorial inwardly prefers truth to falsehood; and that they would fain displace books which perpetuate mystery, despotism and old fogyism by those which advocate intelligibility; which demonstrate how to achieve *actual liberty;* which show how abominably the sexual relations have hitherto been fooled with, and how to remedy that and every other evil. But whoever dares not say so in a straightforward manner evidently has not yet, as "*The World*" says that I have, made the grand discovery that "honesty is the best policy."

" *The World* " evidently does not discern the signs of the times. It libels the intelligence of the age, and underrates nineteenth century advancement in not daring to approve my course and recommend my publications, without *feigning* to be doing the contrary.

Does " *The World* " expect or desire to be believed sincere by those whose opinions it values, and whose judgments it respects, when it affirms that the renowned " *Decameron* " *of Boccaccio*,\* and the world-famous " *Confessions* " *of Jean Jacques Rousseau*, are works of " slender literary merit ?" " *The Confessions*," says Lord Brougham, " is the greatest triumph ever won by diction."

Does " *The World* " sincerely wish it to be understood that it judges Dryden, Ovid, and Johannes Secundus to be authors of " slender literary merit ?"

Nor shall " *The World* " excuse itself for advertising my publications " *gratis*," under the pretext of exposing me for attempting to bribe it to puff them. At the risk of appearing ungrateful, even, I assert, upon my honor, that I never, either " anonymously " or " personally," offered, or instigated to be offered, pay to *any one* for " puffing " or praising my books ; that I knew nothing whatever concerning a recent " *Puff Gratis*," both of myself and my books, until I read it in " *The World*." When I cannot do business except by such contemptible methods, I will retire ; or, at least, be consistent enough to publish only such books as are conceived in falsehood, and can best be palmed off through corruption.

I am duly grateful to " *The World* " for its evident *good intentions* toward me as a publisher of " Books which *are* Books," and which are reliable, or " without suppression ;" and, in return, I will give it a piece of information. Mankind, with the exception of the pitiably unintelligent, are now so sick of mystery, and its superincumbent political, social, and moral inefficiency and abomination, that they simply endure these, *together with the gammon which hypocritical cowards perpetrate in consequence thereof*, because they do not well see how to get rid of them : they patiently *suffer* these, whilst waiting for the triumph of the intelligible and satisfactory religion of science, and its corresponding governmental or social art. If you have anything useful, or which, after duly considering, you deem useful *and practical*, to offer on religious and social subjects, or, if you wish to direct attention to useful books in relation thereto, and guide the *thinking* public to *where such books are sold*, let what you *say* indicate *directly* what you *mean*. All but downright fools will like you the better for it, and, what is of vastly more importance to yourself, or *should be*, you will thus *justly* secure your own respect and esteem.

If we *really have* an inquisition in this country ; a power somehow lurking in *our* social structure—in *our* " model republic," which overrides its own " *free* " " *Constitution*," vetoes Protestantism, and belies all our boasts of liberty ; a power before whom reformers, or *their friends*, have *cause* to quail, and falter and prevaricate, as " The World " seemingly does, measures cannot be too promptly taken to eliminate that abomination, to purge our democratic republic of what, to it, is immeasurably more humiliating and disgraceful than it can be in Spain, or in any country where civilization has not advanced to Protestantism and its correlative, the " *elective franchise*."

---

\* Such writers as Ben Jonson, Dryden, Moliere, and even Shakspeare, have, *surreptitiously*, I am sorry to say, taken Boccaccio for their model ; and Roscoe, and even Milton, seem at a loss for terms strong enough to express their admiration of the genius which conceived " *The Decameron*."